Getting Lost in God

How to Let Jesus Pursue, Heal, and Satisfy You

Janelle M. Andonie

CLAY BRIDGES
PRESS

Getting Lost in God
How to Let Jesus Pursue, Heal, and Satisfy You

ISBN-13: 978-1-939815-85-9
eISBN-13: 978-1-939815-91-0

Special Sales: Most Clay Bridges titles are available in special quantity discounts. Custom imprinting or excerpting can also be done to fit special needs. Contact Clay Bridges at Info@ClayBridgesPress.com.

I want to dedicate this book to the single woman who has the desire to get married. To the single woman who thinks there is no hope out there. To the single woman who is tired of running on empty. To the single woman who feels like there are no good men left. To the single woman who has been measuring her worth and value by men, rejections, and breakups.

To the single woman who is done wasting time. To the single woman who is ready for the real thing, ready to be pursued by the real man—Jesus. This book is for you. It is God-breathed for you. It is intentional. It has your name on it. Girlie, God sees you and wants you to partner with Him. Do not give up hope. Just surrender all to Him. Let Him meet you. Let Him pursue you. He has living water. Let Him write your love story.

Table of Contents

Prologue

"Do you love me?" God asked.

"I love you, God," I responded.

"Then write my book," He said.

I went home and began writing that in my diary, thinking about how a confirmation from God would be good. I mean, writing a book is a big task. When I finished writing, I noticed I had an entry from January 28, 2019, that I had not completed. Weird, I thought. I went to my phone and looked to see if I had written the entry there since that is usually what happens when I am on the go and later transfer it to my diary. When I found it, the entry said, "I feel like God wants me to write a book for single women." Confirmation.

I want to share a little bit about my journey and what God has taught me throughout my single season. You see, I thought I would be married by 24 and would probably have kids already, but God knew better. I'm sure that if you are reading this book, you also thought you would have been married by now or have a desire to get married in the future. Girlie, I encourage you to partner with the Holy Spirit to go through this book together and let Him remove any blindfolds, misconceptions, or lies you have believed. Let Him minister to you so you can get healthy before you make the commitment of marriage. Invite Him in, and dig deep. Heal from past relationships, and set your standards.

I wrote this book with bold truths, but know that behind these writings are love and the wisdom God has given me. At the end of each chapter, take time to ask God, "What is for me, and what do I need to work on?" Be intentional with Him. This is just a tool to get where you want to be, but only God can take you there. I pray that this book opens your eyes to see your single season differently.

By the time you finish this book, I want you to realize that Jesus is the only One who can love you with a radical love. If you are rooted and grounded in Him, you won't need another person to make you happy. I am praying for your journey and am confident that if God placed the desire for marriage in you, He will bring it to pass. Grab your Bible, a pen, and a notebook, and be encouraged!

CHAPTER ONE

Seasons during Your Singleness

I have found that there are different seasons during our singleness: the waiting season, the hiding season, and the counterfeit season. You may not go through all of them, and the seasons might have a different order. Everyone's journey is different. But my purpose is to encourage you where you are now and prepare you if you do enter another season.

The Waiting Season

Caleb, one of the spies Moses sent to scout the Promised Land before taking possession of it, faithfully and wholeheartedly waited 45 years to enter it. How many of us get weary after waiting one month, one year, or five years for God's promises to come to pass? Don't get me wrong—waiting is hard. But what if the waiting season had a purpose? You see, sometimes we are just not ready for the promise. I have learned that God uses waiting periods to help build our character and our faith and to give us what we need to handle and take care of God's promises to us.

Don't give up, and don't lose heart. He sees you, and He is *in* the waiting. In the meantime, draw near to Him, be open to what He wants to show and teach you, and enjoy the journey. You don't have to wait around for a husband before you do things you've always wanted to do, such as travel, buy a house or a car, or even move to another state or country. If God is telling you to move but you worry that you might miss meeting your husband, believe me, you will not ruin God's plans. He already knows how everything will work out. I believe God has an appointment time for everything, so there is nothing you can do to make it happen more quickly. But remain confident in this, the promises God has for you will not fail. What is for you, no one can take away. Consider Joshua and the Israelites. After seven years of battling for the Promised Land, God fulfilled His promise and gave each tribe (except the Levites) a piece of land.

> *Not a single one of all the good promises the* LORD
> *had given to the family of Israel was left unfulfilled;*
> *everything he had spoken came true.*
> —Josh. 21:45 NLT

Another example is in Numbers 23. Balak, the Moabite king, was trying to get the prophet Balaam to curse Israel since they were residing on his plains. He tried to do that three times by changing locations, but Balaam continued to bless Israel since God had already ordained Israel to be blessed. You see, Balaam was in tune with what God was saying. When Balak asked Balaam what God had said, Balaam responded like this:

> *God is not a man, so he does not lie. He is not human,*
> *so he does not change his mind. Has he ever spoken*
> *and failed to act? Has he ever promised and not*
> *carried it through?*
> —Num. 23:19 NLT

You see, what God has promised and appointed, no one can thwart. But how many of us start doubting God's sovereignty? "God, I know you promised I would get married, but you are telling me to go on a dating fast for two years. How is that going to happen?" Girlie, if God is telling you to go on a dating fast or go off online dating, His previous promise that you will get married still stands as long as you walk in obedience. His Word says that obedience is better than sacrifice (1 Sam. 15:22). And yes, I know obedience is hard, but if it were easy, everyone would do it. You have to remember that you are not everyone. You were created for a purpose, and if you die to yourself, yield to the Holy Spirit, and follow Him, you will make the right decisions. Meditate on the verses below and guard them in your heart so you can be encouraged regarding God's sovereignty and faithfulness.

> *Sovereign LORD, you are God! Your covenant is trustworthy, and you have promised these good things to your servant.*
>
> —2 Sam. 7:28

> *Praise be to the LORD, who has given rest to his people Israel just as he promised. Not one word has failed of all the good promises he gave through his servant Moses.*
>
> —1 Kings 8:56

> *For the word of the LORD is right and true; he is faithful in all he does.*
>
> —Ps. 33:4

> *Every word of God is flawless; he is a shield to those who take refuge in him.*
>
> —Prov. 30:5

> *The grass withers and the flowers fall, but the word of our God endures forever.*
>
> —Isa. 40:8

Heaven and earth will pass away, but my words will never pass away.

—Matt. 24:35

For no word from God will ever fail.

—Luke 1:37

If we are faithless, he remains faithful—for he cannot deny himself.

—2 Tim. 2:13 ESV

The Hiding Season

Another season during singleness is the hiding season. When I was in college, I was never asked out by a guy. I admit I was on a mission to graduate with a 4.0 GPA, so the library or my dorm was the place to be. But the fact was I was not ready to go into a relationship. Even after I graduated and moved to Dallas for my master's program, I was rarely asked out the first year and then seldom the second year.

If you are not being asked out, it does not mean you are defective or that something is wrong with you. The Bible says in Ecclesiastes 3:1 that there is a season and a time for everything. When you are in this season of hiding, it is time to remove the enemy's lies and plant the Word of God in your heart so that in due season, you can reap a harvest. I find that sometimes we are in this season when we still have to heal from a past relationship. For example, if you have not healed from hurts by a past boyfriend or from your father, how can you consider someone for marriage? At that point, your views of relationships and marriage are not healthy. You don't have a healthy role model of what relationships should look like. How loving is God that He is pushing pause in the dating stage of your life so you can prevent future hurts! He wants you to partner and get in agreement with Him to heal from those wounds and become a healthier version of yourself.

Another reason you may be in this season is because your identity may be rooted in the lies of the world. If your identity is not 100 percent in Jesus, you are not standing on a steady foundation. You have not tapped into your true worth and value. You have not had a revelation of the royalty you are. Instead, you are fickle, unstable, and easily moved. If you entered a relationship, you would probably end up compromising your true value. You would be more concerned about pleasing that person or looking a certain way than evaluating if they have the right attributes for you. Think about it. Are you basing your value on what people think or say about you? Are you basing your value on how beautiful you look on a date? Are you basing your value on what you do for a living? Your successes? All your degrees? If your identity and worth do not come from above, you will not have a successful relationship or marriage.

Let go of trying to control the seasons and recognize that you have a good Father who cares for you. Believe me, I've been there. I am a type A person who always has a plan and loves to control things. God had to shake me once about my timing versus His. He told me, "Relinquishing control over a desire does not mean it won't happen or that you have to lose hope. It means to let go of your expectations so you can receive something greater." How good is that? He wants us to let go of what we think should happen and how it should happen so He can do something greater in due season. Let us take Him out of the box, or even better, let's just get rid of the box. Girlie, if you keep your eyes on God, He will give you what you need at the proper time.

> *The eyes of all look to you,*
> *and you give them their food in due season.*
> *You open your hand;*
> *you satisfy the desire of every living thing.*
> —Ps. 145:15–16 ESV

This is the perfect season to grow closer to God and know Him intimately. It is not a season of complaining about how no one asks you out or how long singleness is taking. Do not be like the Israelites who still complained even after witnessing God's mighty hand and His goodness over and over. You see, when you complain, you are doubting God's goodness in your life. I don't know about you, but I never want to be found doubting my Father's goodness or intentions toward me. Doubt shows a lack of faith, which the Bible clearly tells us does not please God.

The Counterfeit Season

If you are not in the hiding season, you might be in the counterfeit season. In that season, you typically come across a lot of guys who seem like good prospects, but when you look closer, you know they are not the real thing. They might go to church, take their Bible, and worship, but after leaving church, they live a different life.

Some counterfeits are easy to spot. For example, if a guy is not a believer, he is still a counterfeit even if he does everything right or you're attracted to him. I once had a guy from my apartment building approach me and say, "You're beautiful. I've always seen you around. Can I get your number?" We texted for a bit, and he said he would get back to me after a trip he was taking. I sensed he was a player and had already made up my mind that he was not what I was looking for, but my friends advised me to give it a try since my reasoning wasn't logical. After returning, he was still vague and unintentional about getting together. When he added me on social media, I did what any Christian girl would do and looked at his followers to see if he was following any Christian speakers. The answer—no—matched my gut instinct. Instead, he was following the accounts of girls who were showing more than they needed to.

After three weeks, he finally asked to meet up, and guess what the text said? "Let me know if you are free, and I can bring a bottle of wine over." My reaction: run away. Lesson one: No godly,

Christian man who is serious about getting to know you will invite himself to your apartment with wine. That screams booty call all around, especially since I barely knew him. Lesson two, ladies, is to follow the leading of the Holy Spirit. It is important to distinguish between emotional decisions and Holy Spirit nudges. When the Holy Spirit is speaking, most of the time it does not make sense. For example, this guy was educated, had a job, and was handsome and charismatic, but the Holy Spirit said no even when the world would say yes. Lesson three is to make sure you don't believe everything a guy tells you. Just because he makes himself seem great by what he says does not mean he is actually walking it. Test and see if his actions match his words.

So what happened? I followed that Holy Spirit nudge. I knew I had an assignment to write this book and empower women, which was already hard since I was working a full-time job, serving, and keeping up with my health and friendships. Why would I add a distraction in my life and put myself through an empty relationship? I ended up texting him the truth: "Thanks for the offer, but I don't think we are looking for the same thing." Don't get me wrong. I'm not saying you can't be friendly and show someone the love of Christ, but why date a guy when you know you don't have the same focus? Listen to what the Apostle Paul says:

> Do not be unequally yoked with unbelievers. For what partnership has righteousness with lawlessness? Or what fellowship has light with darkness?
>
> —2 Cor. 6:14 ESV

Samson was in a similar situation. He basically taught Dating Gone Wrong 101. Samson was a Nazirite who was given supernatural strength by God to help deliver Israel from the Philistines. Even though he had the potential to be used greatly by God, he chose to be led by sensuality and used his gift unwisely. For example, he chose to marry a Philistine woman who did not share his same beliefs. On top of that, he chose her based on her looks.

> *His father and mother objected. "Isn't there even one woman in our tribe or among all the Israelites you could marry?" they asked. "Why must you go to the pagan Philistines to find a wife?" But Samson told his father, "Get her for me! She looks good to me."*
> —Judges 14:3 NLT

Wow! Samson let his *eyes* choose his bride. If we are being honest, how many of us try to do that? We let our eyes and hormones decide the man we will spend the rest of our lives with. We let our eyes decide who is supposed to partner with us in this covenant called marriage. We let our eyes decide the person we are going to serve with and who will come alongside us. We see a guy, and even if he is not a Christian, we still think we can make it work. We think, "I can easily make him go to church with me." But what does the Word of God say about using our eyes as the decision-maker?

> *Charm is deceptive, and beauty does not last; but a woman who fears the LORD will be greatly praised.*
> —Prov. 31:30 NLT

This verse also applies to men. Just because a guy is attractive does not automatically qualify him as a potential husband. There is nothing wrong with marrying someone you are attracted to, but looks shouldn't be the decisive factor. Just think about it. If you want your marriage to last, it has to be built on the firm foundation of Jesus Christ. If you build your marriage on a flaky foundation such as beauty and charm, your marriage will shake and crumble. Girlie, God is a loving Father. If it's in His instruction book, it's because He loves you and knows best.

It is crucial for your husband to have an actual relationship with the most high God. Think about a person you love, such as your mom. What if your husband didn't like her and you couldn't mention your mom around him. That would be so hard! But it's just a glimpse of how difficult a relationship with an unbeliever would be. Imagine how much harder a relationship would be if you couldn't talk about how much you love God, how God has helped you, or how God is speaking to you. If God has become your sustenance, there is no way you could be with someone who does not know Him.

You might be asking, "What if this guy does love the Lord?" That is when it gets a little tricky. This guy may be a strong believer and have a relationship with God, but if it does not flow easily, you will know. What do I mean by "flow easily"? It means you can't have a conversation with him. There are constant disagreements. You don't have fun with him. Life does not seem better with him than without him. You do not have similar values or a direction of where you want your life to go. Girlie, if you are just attracted to him and do not have a friendship as a basis, take time to explore whether you have fun around him and if a friendship is possible. If he looks perfect but there is one thing you do not feel peace about, pay attention to it. Ask yourself the hard questions. Why don't I feel peace about it? Is it a Holy Spirit nudge or just emotions? Can I still love him if that specific thing never changes?

This situation happened to me. I met a guy who seemed perfect. He loved the Lord, saw my inner beauty, and seemed to be living for God. He talked about how he had left everything for Jesus and moved to Dallas. He seemed to have a plan and have his life together. He even hinted several times how I would be his wife. I was a little taken aback that he was so straightforward and certain, but at the same time, I was excited and attracted to him and his relationship with Jesus.

In the midst of all this, I was also feeling confused, scared, and overwhelmed. I felt like it was too good to be true, but I was also unsure. I felt like I was slow in catching up with God since this guy *knew* I was his wife and I hadn't gotten the memo from God. In the end, I was not feeling at peace and had that Holy Spirit nudge, so I ended it. I didn't have any good reason other than I was not feeling right about it. I later found out that he was asking multiple girls out and was growing distant from church community groups that help members be accountable for their actions. Girlie, the Holy Spirit is your best guide here. Even when others around you start questioning your decisions and accusing you of being too picky, stand your ground and wait for the Lord. His plans for you are good. Would you take Him at His word?

You get to a point in life where you are done with counterfeits and only want the real thing. Believe me, I've been there—the Netflix-and-chill guy, the come-over-with-wine guy, the you-are-my-wife guy, the I'm-not-sure guy, the sender-of-nude-pictures guy, and the list goes on. What do they all have in common? They are not after your heart. They are not intentional. And they are not there to pursue and love you faithfully. They are being led by their hormones and fleeting emotions. You don't have time for boys. You don't have time to be arguing about why your boyfriend does not want to go to church, why he is texting other women, or why he is liking other girls' pictures on Instagram. If you are looking for marriage, I hope you have a greater vision than a man who commits to a relationship halfheartedly. Marriage is a reflection of how God loves the church. It is about unifying gifts and having a mission to go out, serve people, and make Jesus known, whether in your job, on the mission field, or raising your babies as a stay-at-home mom.

You have been bought with a price and are royalty in God's eyes. You are worthy of a man who is going to treat you with love and respect you. A man who is going to love you as God loves the church and challenge you with the Word of God. A man who has a vision and a mission in his life and can direct the way of the marriage. A man who is actually working, has an income, and can support you.

I'm not saying he should be the sole breadwinner, but he should at least have a job or be studying to eventually get one.

I encourage you to abstain from dating a guy out of boredom or loneliness. Nothing good will come out of it. Instead, focus on your emotional and physical health as well as getting vision for your purpose in life. We will discuss these topics in the next few chapters.

Ending Prayer

God, thank You for loving me so much that You even ordain the seasons I am in. Thank You for giving me exactly what I need in this season. I pray that You would give me the strength and wisdom to learn and grasp everything You have for me in this chapter of my life. Do not let me waste a season by desiring to be in the next season. I calm and quiet my soul and choose to live in the present and in Your timeline. As long as You are with me, I can delight in wherever I am. Amen.

CHAPTER TWO

Learn to Hear from God

Understanding how we can hear from God is one of my favorite topics. I used to doubt my ability to hear from God since He had never spoken to me audibly. If you are in the same place, I encourage you to be confident. God longs to speak to you. He longs to comfort you when you are in pain. He longs to speak truth to you when you are consumed by lies. He longs to show you your value when you feel as if you aren't enough. And He loves to guide you when you don't know your next step.

I've found that God speaks in different ways to each person. Let's walk through some of the key methods God uses to communicate with us.

1. Audible Voice

Speaking in an audible voice was God's most common method of speaking to people in the days of the Bible. We see how God spoke audibly to Abraham, Moses, and even Saul (later Paul). The mind-blowing part of Saul's story is that he hated God and was on a mission to kill believers, but God still spoke to him. Saul's story also shows God's mercy and love for unbelievers. Even if you are closed off to God, He can still show himself. In the end, Saul's name changed to Paul, and he was greatly used by God, going on to write many books of the New Testament. You see, God's voice is so full of love, truth, and grace that if you hear it, you cannot deny His deity and sovereignty. This form of God speaking is not as common today, but that does not mean that it does not happen.

2. Angels and Visitations

God can also speak through angels or visitations. Mary encountered an angel when Gabriel appeared to her and informed her that she would be having a baby—Jesus. In those days, visitations from angels were normal, but now, visitations would be a shock to most people. If you think about it, though, how much more faith do we exercise to believe in God, even though we haven't experienced physical encounters? Don't be disappointed or believe there is something wrong with you if a visitation has not happened to you. God Himself tells us in the Bible that "blessed are those who have not seen and yet have believed" (John 20:29 ESV).

3. The Bible

I believe the Bible is one of the easiest ways for God to speak to us, but it is often overlooked. When we are looking for direction or an answer, we tend to go to a friend, parent, or sibling. God wants you to go to Him first. Why are you asking a friend who has skewed priorities and isn't living a life you would want to emulate? Why not go to a God-breathed book? You see, God spoke, and His servants wrote—that is how the Bible was written. So when you read it, read it as if God were speaking to you. It is personal for you and for me. When you read it, God knows exactly what you need that day and is faithful to highlight it. The Bible itself states how the Word of God is "living and active" (Heb. 4:12 AMP). What does God mean? He means that every time you read the Bible, even if you are reading the same verse, you get a new revelation. Why? Because the Word is God, and God is always speaking. He is intentional.

> *For the word of God is living and active* and *full of power [making it operative, energizing, and effective].*
> *It is sharper than any two-edged sword, penetrating as far as the division of the soul and spirit [the completeness of a person], and of both joints and marrow [the deepest parts of our nature], exposing* and *judging the very thoughts and intentions of the heart.*
>
> —Heb. 4:12 AMP

God's Word is what purifies us. It is what God uses to correct us in a loving way to look more like Him.

In the New Testament, God also spoke through Jesus, who often spoke in parables. Parables are simple stories with a moral lesson, but the meaning of some parables can be difficult to understand. Why do you think that is? God wants us to be fully committed. He wants a relationship with us. He is full of mysteries, and He does not reveal Himself or His secrets lightly. You have to dig for them. So as you read the Bible, be intentional and look for patterns, repeated words, and the meanings of words. Do not get discouraged if at first you can't understand a story. Try changing translations, but most importantly, ask God. He will be faithful to reveal His mysteries to you. His Word says that if we seek, we will find Him, and if we knock, He will answer. Be intentional and expectant.

4. Thoughts

God can also speak by placing thoughts in your mind. Be careful, though. It is important to test every thought with the Word of God. Does the idea align with scripture? Is it based on fears or emotions? If it does not align with the Word of God, it is not from Him, and it is important to bring that thought in alignment with Christ. The Bible teaches us how to do that.

> *We demolish arguments and every pretension that*
> *sets itself up against the knowledge of God, and we*
> *take captive every thought to make it obedient to*
> *Christ.*
>
> —2 Cor. 10:5

You have the authority to cast down any thought and set it under God's feet. Just because you have a thought does not mean it is true. That is why it is important to be constantly renewing your mind by planting the Word of God in your heart. When God places a thought in your head, it aligns with scripture, and it is life-giving. It is there to edify, comfort, or exhort you in love.

God often speaks to me this way and once gave me a sentence for a coworker. While she was translating what I was saying to one of my client's parents, I was staring at her. Suddenly I heard in my mind, "She has so much favor." After finishing our work, I told her what I had heard, and she shared how she was waiting for a scholarship to continue studying for her degree. After hearing the phrase, she felt much more confident that God would make a way. The next day, she told me that someone had donated money, and her tuition had been paid. Thank you, Jesus!

Some of you might be asking, how did I know I was hearing from God? First, I was not thinking about anything when the thought popped into my head. That is usually how I know God is speaking. Second, I would have never thought it on my own. Third, the idea aligned with scripture—as we walk rightly with God, He does give us favor. So after testing the thought, I knew God had spoken it since He wanted to bring comfort to His daughter.

God has also placed Bible verses in my mind. For example, one time in college, I was stressed about a lab exam I'd just taken, feeling unsure about some of the answers I'd chosen. As I was walking to the parking lot, this verse came to my mind: "The Lord will perfect *that which* concerns me" (Ps. 138:8 NKJV). I hadn't been thinking about that verse, but it was exactly what I needed. It was God telling me, "Stop worrying, I got this." Situations like these are why it is crucial to read the Bible and store verses in your heart and mind. If they are not rooted in your heart, how will God bring them to remembrance?

5. Songs and TV Shows

God can also speak through secular situations. Friends have often told me stories of God speaking to them through TV shows or the plot of a movie. Sometimes, I've hopped in my car and heard a song that described exactly what I was going through. God can use any moment He chooses to remind us that He sees us and knows exactly what we are going through.

6. Dreams

God can also speak through dreams. We see that in the story of Joseph when God gave him dreams and also the ability to interpret them. To help remember your dreams, leave a notepad beside your bed so you can write them down as soon as you wake up. Then ask God what the dream means. Sometimes, dreams are pretty straightforward, but others have to be deciphered. I work as a home health dietitian, and I once had a dream about sexual assault happening at a patient's home. The next day, I went into the office, and one of my coworkers mentioned how there was a possibility that drugs were being used in that patient's home. Some of the areas I go to are not the safest, and I took that as a warning from God to pray before going to that house. The next time I went to that house, the young mom took me to what seemed like a small basement where she and her two kids resided. Thankfully, I followed that Holy Spirit nudge and prayed, and God protected me. You see, God uses dreams to warn us or inform us of things to come. If you rarely dream, ask God to begin speaking to you in dreams. He is faithful.

7. Other People

God also uses the body of Christ to speak to us, whether it be a word of knowledge, wisdom, or prophecy. A word of knowledge is when God tells someone something about you that they could not have known unless you had told them. Some examples would be your name, where you are from, or something you are going through. A word of wisdom is when a person tells you how to deal with a certain situation. Finally, a prophetic word is one that speaks about the future and is given to comfort, exhort, or edify you. One example of this is the time I was prophesied a new car in the fall of 2018, and in January 2019, I had a new car. It is important to always test prophetic words with scripture to see if the idea aligns with God's Word. It is also good to save prophetic words and keep meditating on them since they may not happen instantly. God has His own timing.

A great example of when God gave me a word of knowledge for someone was when I was in a prayer and worship service at my church. During the service, I was watching a lady worship very passionately, and a thought popped into my mind: "Her name is _____, and she has a prodigal son." The thought surprised me since I did not know her. I waited until the service was finished and then went up to her to share what God had given me. She was moved and affirmed what I said. At the end of our conversation, I was able to pray for her and encourage her that her son would come to know Jesus. Girlie, the more you step out when you hear from God, the more He will speak. Be faithful in the little things so He can reward you with more.

What about Feelings?

Sometimes we might think our feelings indicate what God is saying. The truth is feelings can be misleading, but I believe God can speak through a sense of peace. My disclaimer is to always question your feelings. For example, sometimes we can feel afraid of making a decision, so naturally, we don't feel peace about it. But just because you feel some fear does not mean the decision is against God's will. Most of the time, God calls us to do things out of our comfort zone, ability, and strength. Just because it's hard does not always mean it's not God. His Word says that in our weakness, He is strong (2 Cor. 12:10). If you fear a certain decision that you think God is calling you to, ask why and dig deeper. For example, I felt like God was asking me to write this book. I felt peace about the decision, but I also felt hesitant and scared, and I questioned who would even read the book. Why? First of all, I've never been good at writing. You see, English is my second language, so sometimes it is hard to put thoughts together in an articulate and nonredundant way. Second, I am not a well-known author, I have never been in a relationship, and the truths I planned to share in this book were not the standard of this world. Instead, they are a way to live set apart for God in this dating world. But even though I hesitated and felt unqualified, I started writing the book. I placed my lack of qualifications aside and did what God had told me to do, stepping out in faith. Why? Because it is God who qualifies me in the end. And I've learned that this life is not about me but about bringing glory to God by letting Him use my story as healing for other women.

Another example is when I had wanted to serve in the prophetic ministry at my church for almost two years but had put it off because of fear. I dug into my feelings and spotted the lie—I doubted if God would come through and speak to me. You see, the enemy will place lies and fears in your mind to stop you from fulfilling God's calling for your life. It is your responsibility to examine your feelings, expose the truth, and step out in faith.

I am not saying that feelings are bad. God created them. But if you let them rule your decisions, they can become dangerous. We are called to live by the Spirit and not by our feelings. So when you sense God is calling you to an action but your feelings are not obeying you, speak to them. The Bible says that we have life or death in the power of our tongues and that God has given us power to demolish strongholds and every power of darkness. When you start speaking to your feelings and declaring the opposite of what you feel, your feelings will follow your words. Girlie, you have to speak truth until you start believing it.

If you are just starting this journey and hearing from God is new to you, here are some steps to get better at hearing His voice:

- Ask God to speak to you and help you be more attuned to His voice.
- Have conversations with Him during the day, and study how He tends to speak to you.
- Be intentional by asking questions. An easy way to do this is to grab a notebook, write down questions, and write what God is speaking to you.
- Step out in faith by asking God to give you a word for someone else. I know this sounds scary, but God is faithful when you step out and have faith that He will follow through. I've found that sometimes God only gives me a single word for someone, but when I step out and share it, He downloads the meaning of it as I am speaking. What do I mean by *downloads*? I mean that God speaks more about the situation, and I am able to minister to that person in a deeper way. Think about when you get an email with an attachment. At first, you only know the name of the attachment. Once you click on it to download it, you are able to have access to the full body of information. But if you are not obedient with sharing the small, how will God show you the big? Girlie, God wants your faith, and by only revealing part by part, He humbles us and reminds us that He is the One to be praised and not ourselves. We are merely listening. You see, the Bible says we walk by faith and not by sight. Just because you don't have the whole message figured out does not mean you should not share it. He is faithful to meet you outside of the boat as you step out and walk on the water with Him.

The Bible states, "My sheep listen to my voice; I know them, and they follow me" (John 10:27). You are His sheep, so you don't have to strive to hear His voice. If you have not made Jesus your Lord and Savior and would like to have this intimate relationship with Him, today is your day. He loves you and wants to be there for you. You don't have to do life on your own. He can be your healer, counselor, friend, provider of strength, and so much more. If you are ready to commit to His Lordship and make Him your Lord and Savior, say this prayer: "God, I accept you as my Lord and Savior. I am done living in my own strength and following my own desires. I invite you into my life and give you control over my life." If you said that prayer, congratulations, and welcome to the family. The best is yet to come.

Now, pray the prayer below and then ask God the questions that follow, writing down what you hear Him speaking over you.

Ending Prayer

Thank You, God, for sending your Son to die for me. Thank You for letting me come into Your presence boldly and confidently. Thank You for allowing me to be in a relationship with You, talk to You, and hear from You. I pray that I am sensitive to Your voice and that I do not get distracted with outside voices. I declare that I am Your sheep, and I hear Your voice. The Word says that whatever I ask in prayer, I will receive if I have faith. So I thank You for what You are already doing, God. Amen.

I read John 10 today ↘
12.6.21

- God, what are You speaking over me today?
- God, what is Your favorite thing about me?
- God, what Bible book do You want me to study this month?
- God, what do You want me to focus on in this season?

CHAPTER THREE

Make Prayer a Priority

What Is Prayer?

According to the *Merrian-Webster Dictionary*, prayer is an address (such as a petition) to God or a god in word or thought. Even though I agree that prayer can be a petition, deep down I truly believe that praying is simply having a conversation with your Father. It can either manifest itself by giving thanks, asking for help, talking to Him during the day, or even praying in the Spirit. Most of my life, I was self-conscious about praying out loud since I did not know the "right" words to use. But when you talk with your Father, it does not have to be elaborate. Consider a toddler, for example. As they learn to talk, they cut out syllables from words. When they try to speak, their parents get very excited. They rejoice since their little one is *making an effort* to communicate with them. Parents don't chastise their children for mispronouncing words or using incorrect grammar. Look at Matthew 6:7, where Jesus teaches us how to pray. He says, "And when you pray, do not keep on babbling like pagans, for they think they will be heard because of their many words." Girlie, He just wants a relationship with you.

It is important for you to actually have faith when you are praying. The Bible tells us that without faith, we cannot please God. Look at 1 John 5:14–15: "This is the confidence we have in approaching God: that if we ask anything according to his will, he hears us. And if we know that he hears us—whatever we ask—we know that we have what we asked of him." James 1:6 also addresses the same idea: "But when you ask, you must believe and not doubt, because the one who doubts is like a wave of the sea, blown and tossed by the wind." If you are lacking faith, ask God for it.

The Bible also gives us the recipe for faith. The key ingredient is hearing the Word of God. Ask yourself, "What am I listening to every day?" Are you listening to people complain all day? Gossip? TV shows? Secular music? To build up your faith, you have to immerse yourself in the Word of God, listen to other people's testimonies, and listen to sermons. Stop trying to produce faith with the wrong ingredients—it is as futile as hoping to bake a cake without flour, eggs, and milk.

Once you've built up your faith, approach God's throne boldly with thanksgiving. Either thank Him for what He has done in the past or what He is going to do in your future. The Bible says that God inhabits the praises of His people, and as you praise Him in thanksgiving, you'd better believe He will come. Once you are there, submit your request to Him, and believe you have received it. The Bible promises us that it will come to pass (Mark 11:24).

You might be asking, "Janelle, what if I do not have the motivation to pray?" Girlie, I've been there! Sometimes, we lack motivation when we feel like what we are asking for is too impossible for God (as if there is such a thing). But let's dig deeper. Why do we feel that way? I've noticed that I lack motivation when:

1. I am not walking in the Spirit but in the flesh.
2. I am not agreeing with God's Word.
3. I have not built up my faith to pray.

The good news is that you do not have to do the work—you just have to agree with what God told you and hope for things not seen yet. Do not let unbelief get in the way. Simply because a situation seems impossible for you does not mean it is impossible for God. Your Father specializes in impossible situations.

Maybe for you, though, praying seems pointless since you believe that God is sovereign, and it's up to Him whether I will ever get married. Yes, God is sovereign, but He is a loving God who has given us free will. Girlie, He cherishes your prayers. Revelation 5:8 says that heaven has "golden bowls full of incense, which are the prayers of God's people." How mind-blowing is that? God actually stores all our prayers. You see, they are a fragrant incense to Him, and He intentionally stores them. He longs to hear from you. Do not hold back!

I've also learned to focus and be intentional when I spend time with God. When we read the Word, worship, pray, and check off everything on our list, are we leaving room for God to speak? Are we having a monologue instead of a conversation? I've noticed that sometimes I can spend one hour doing all these *things*, but I didn't even ask God *what He thinks* about a situation or what He wants to do through me that day. I encourage you to be a woman who does not get your value in *doing actions* but in *having an actual relationship* with your Creator. Let's all be women who delight in hearing God more than checking quiet time off our list. Let's be a Mary in this Martha-world.

Finally, it is important to be intentional, to set a time to fellowship with God and pray. Once you've made up your mind that you are going all in, the enemy will send distractions to make you feel as if you have no time to pray. I encourage you to set a time each day and stick with it. Put it on your calendar. Since the enemy is threatened, he will not roll out the red carpet once you decide to be intentional. The Bible says that the enemy prowls like a lion looking for someone to devour. So when you are the weakest, enter the throne room.

For me, when I get home and feel tired and drained from the day, I lie on my floor and soak in worship music. Even if I feel weak, my spirit longs to spend time with my God. While soaking in declarations of truth, my faith and strength start to increase, and then I am able to start thanking God even if it is for the silliest, smallest things. By the end of my time, I am praying like never before and even praying in the Spirit. Look at Romans 8:26–27:

> *In the same way, the Spirit helps us in our weakness. We do not know what we ought to pray for, but the Spirit himself intercedes for us through wordless groans. And he who searches our hearts knows the mind of the Spirit, because the Spirit intercedes for God's people in accordance with the will of God.*

You see, when you are weak, He is strong. When you can't even think straight, He is better able to use you and pray through you since your ways and mindsets are out of the way.

I pray that God would reveal the power of fellowshipping with Him and that you would have a deeper revelation of His heart for you. I pray that you would not feel obligated to spend time and pray with your Father, but that prayer would come as a deep longing to get to know Him better. Girlie, remember, He longs to hear from you.

Ending Prayer

Thank You, God, for giving us a desire to be in fellowship with You all day. Thank You for letting us come boldly to Your throne and approach You without condemnation. I pray that You would give me childlike faith so I can believe what I pray.

CHAPTER FOUR

Let Jesus Pursue You

Let Jesus pursue you. Interesting, huh? Some of you might be saying, "How would Jesus pursue me? I know He's my Savior, but I don't see Him as a pursuer." Girlie, how will you know how a man should pursue you if you have not let Jesus pursue you? He is your Creator. He knows you. He can satisfy every longing you have. Not only that, but He knows how to love you *well*. And how will you love someone well if you have not had a revelation of God's love for you? In 1 John 4:19, the Bible tells us that "we love because He first loved us." If we want to be able to fully love someone else, we have to first let God love us and reveal to us our worth and value.

However, God will not force His fellowship on you. Revelation 3:20 (NKJV) says "Behold, I stand at the door and knock. If anyone hears My voice and opens the door, I will come in to him and eat with him, and he with Me." You see, God is a gentleman. He knocks at the door of your heart, waiting for you to answer. He calls for you and waits patiently. He has had the key to your heart since He *made* you, but He does not enter without your permission. Girlie, it is your decision to let Him come in and give Him access to the deepest parts of your soul and mind. His heart is to fellowship with you. Why do you think He created Adam and Eve? He created them to have communion with them. The Bible also reveals to us how God's thoughts concerning us outnumber the grains of sand. Imagine that! He is constantly thinking about you and waiting for you to reach out to Him.

For me, I got to the point where I really fell in love with God. I would be excited to come back from work because I knew I would get to spend time with Him. Sometimes, on Friday or Saturday nights, I would go on date nights with Him that consisted of grocery shopping, cooking dinner while listening to worship music, and fellowshipping with Him. At times, I served dinner and then forgot to eat because I had more hunger for worship. The first time that happened, I was worshiping while cooking, and when I sat down to eat, I just wanted to weep at His feet. I asked myself, "How come I just want to cry and worship all day?" And I heard God say, "This is what it looks like to fall in love with Me." I was hungrier for the eternal bread of life than the temporary pleasures of food. Imagine if we could live like that every day, every minute, and every second of the day—in tune with His voice, His love, and His pursuit of us.

So what did this pursuit look like? It looked like God always showing up, spoiling me, speaking truth over me, correcting me in love, being a gentleman, respecting me, and loving me unconditionally. On my part, it looked like talking to Him during the day, asking Him questions, worshiping at His feet, reading His Word, and delighting myself in Him. After months of God pursuing me, I finally said "I love you" to Him. This was big for me since I had never said this to Him. Before that, I heard how some people said "I love you" to God and thought, "Wow! That is different. They definitely have a deeper revelation of God than I do. They are definitely all in." I came to realize that this love was birthed from actually spending time with God and being more intimate with Him. Every time I came to Him, He met me. Every time I called unto Him, He was faithful to respond. He was intentional and a gentleman. He was full of truth and wisdom. He reminded me of how much I am worth and loved. He never failed me.

David also tapped into this truth in Psalm 23:6 when he said, "Surely your goodness and love will follow me all the days of my life." David was confident and sure of God's pursuit of him.

You see, God is zealous for you and wants to share memories with you. When God started pursuing me, I sensed Him saying this:

> I want to talk to you. I want to have communion with you. I want you to share these things and memories with Me now. I am jealous and zealous for you. When the time comes, you will be able to share with the person I have for you, who will love you for who you are.

God started preparing my heart for the person He has for me. But if I had not let Him walk me through the process, there would have been a greater chance that I would just settle. Most of the time, we are more concerned about the promise. We say, "God, you promised I would get married." But focusing on the promise and ignoring the process is futile. Either you end up settling or God keeps giving you opportunities to pass through the process again and again.

Girlie, the process allows us to be refined. Think about a diamond. It starts as carbon pieces that need to be put under pressure to become the beautiful diamonds we have today. Without pressure and refinement, the carbon is not ready to be shown off. It is not ready to shine, and it is not able to fulfill its purpose as a diamond. Our journey is similar—it's here where God shows us our worth and builds our character so we can be prepared for that marriage season. The process is where the magic happens. Don't run from it; embrace it!

In this time of pursuit, God will show you how you were *not* created for something small. He will show you your worth and value so you can hold yourself to a high standard. If you are in a state in your life when you would marry the first person who shows you approval or compliments you, I dare you to ask yourself if you have experienced the revelation of the Father's love for you. The Bible says that a wife of noble character is worth far more than rubies. When you have that revelation of the Father's love, you *know* deep inside you, without a shadow of a doubt, how beautiful, valuable, and worthy of pursuit you are. You get to the point where society's pressure, your family's comments, or everyone else's opinions do not move you. You become so in love with having a relationship with Jesus that you trust Him 100 percent. Girlie, God has placed something essential in you with which you get to impact the world, so do not settle for something less than what He has in store. Be strong, take heart, and wait for the LORD (Ps. 27:14).

I'm not saying it will be easy, but God honors your waiting. For example, I've had moments when I wanted to be wanted by someone—moments when I wanted to go on a date, have a meaningful conversation, be known by someone, and be loved unconditionally. During those times, God was faithful to pursue me and remind me that He wanted to spend time with me, have a conversation, or do whatever I wanted to do. Consequently, I started longing to just spend time with Him and worship Him, so I headed home and did just that. I felt like God was telling me in that season, "Janelle, when you feel lonely, remember this: I desire to spend time with you. Come to me. I satisfy." God has never let me down. He has been there in the hard times and in the good times. And the same goes for you. Girlie, He cares. And He sees you.

Now is the perfect time to devote yourself solely to the Lord and stop focusing on finding "the one." Get so lost loving God that the person He has for you will have to be intentional to even find you. Sometimes we are so focused on where that person is or who he could be that we miss the joys of this season with God. How many of us have gone out somewhere and thought only about whether the person God has for us will be there? Or when a guy asks us on a date, we create an entire narrative in our head of how things are going to go.

Without really being conscious of it, that happened to me. A friend kept telling me that my husband would be someone I already knew and someone I had never thought of as more than a friend. Needless to say, I was trying to figure out who it was (as if my friend knew better than God). God had to speak to me through a dream about how much attention I was giving this. In the dream, I had lost my credit card and became obsessed trying to find it. When I woke up, God told me, "This is how I see you right now—obsessing over who your husband is. Stop focusing on who he is. I will provide." You see, God's timing is everything. For me, I wanted to be able to serve God in a bigger way. Deuteronomy 32:30 states, "How could one man chase a thousand, or two put ten thousand to flight?" This verse is about the Israelites fighting against their enemies, but I also believe it portrays a picture of how much more two people—instead of one—joined together in agreement and running toward the same mission under God can accomplish for the kingdom of God. I was also worried I was going to get old and not be as pretty whenever my time came. I wanted to share memories with the person God had for me while I was young and perky. But God told me, "Janelle, your husband will not like you just because of your looks but because of who you are."

Girlie, I believe this truth also applies to you. God has a person who will not only like you because he thinks you are beautiful on the outside but who sees your beauty on the inside. There is no shame in being excited and looking forward to that season, but do not let that eagerness make you miss out on the importance of the present season. I challenge you to consider how you would live if you knew you were going to meet your husband one day. You would enjoy this season. If God has promised you something, He is faithful to fulfill it. He is not a man that He should lie or a human being that He should change His mind. He is your Father, and He knows what's best for you.

I feel like God has given me a picture of how He wants us, His daughters, to love Him. That reminded me of the scene in the movie

33

Pride and Prejudice when Mr. Darcy tells Elizabeth, "You have bewitched me, body and soul, and I love, I love, I love you. I never wish to be parted from you from this day on."[1] This is the kind of love God is looking for. He wants us to wake up, go about our day, and lay down in communion with Him. He wants us to be so in love with Him that we are open and receptive to what He tells us. He wants us to be so close to Him that we can listen to His whispers. And He wants us to count His words as the most trustworthy truth. Girlie, will you accept His invitation to pursue you?

"Marry" this man Jesus. Tell Him "I do" before you tell a human being "I do." Do not go to lesser lovers to find satisfaction. You see, if we can't even commit to Jesus, who is a perfect man, how will we commit to an imperfect man? You need Jesus in your relationship, but most importantly, you need Him in continual communion with you.

Some of you might be thinking, "Yes, I want this kind of love and communion, but how do I get there? Girlie, just talk to Him. A simple "God, I'm open to your pursuit" suffices. He has always been knocking, and He just wants you to open the door to your heart. Be intentional to spend time with Him, and trust me, you won't be disappointed.

Ending Prayer

Jesus, I am open to your pursuit. I want to know You intimately, have a relationship with You, and be fully loved by You before letting a man pursue me. Teach me how I should be treated. Teach me how much I am worth. Teach me how to share and spend time with You. I invite You and give You permission to blow my mind with Your love. Thank You, Lord. Amen.

---

1. *Pride and Prejudice*, directed by Joe Wright, written by Jane Austen (novel) and Deborah Moggach (screenplay), featuring Keira Knightley and Matthew Macfadyen, aired November 23, 2005.

CHAPTER FIVE

Emotional Health

Emotional health is such an important part of your single season. I believe this is the best time to heal from childhood and past relationship wounds. We can also use this time to expose the negative paradigms and strongholds we believe about ourselves. You see, God has given us authority to take thoughts captive and make them obedient to Christ. Just because you believe in a negative way about yourself does not mean it is true, and those thoughts definitely are not from God.

You might be asking, "Janelle, I do have emotional baggage and lies I am believing, but how can I access freedom and break through?" We can find the answer in Luke 24. Look at verses 13 through 33. Jesus met two men who were disappointed that He was not the Messiah. In the midst of being consumed by what everyone was saying, they did not recognize Jesus but decided to eat dinner and spend time with Him. During dinner, Jesus "took bread, gave thanks, broke it and began to give it to them. Then *their eyes were opened and they recognized him*, and he disappeared from their sight" (emphasis added) (Luke 24:30–31). These two men had preconceived ideas of who Jesus was, and it wasn't until they came in contact with Him and spent time with Him that they were able to see who He really was. They even asked each other, "Were not our hearts burning within us while he talked with us on the road and opened the Scriptures to us?" (Luke 24:32). These men could not see who Jesus was until they sat and fellowshipped with Him. You see, the only way our mindsets, lies, and strongholds can come off is by opening the door and spending time with Jesus. He brings clarity. He removes confusion. And He sets us free.

Emotional Health: Family Wounds

Family. We all had one while growing up. Whether a single parent, both parents, grandparents, or an adoptive family—we were all raised by human beings who were far from perfect. They all made mistakes and hurt us in some way. Whether you had a parent who left you or one who was wasn't there for you, you went through some pain. The question is, have you healed from it? Childhood wounds can affect your relationship with God, your friends, and your marriage down the road. If your dad was unfaithful to your mom, you might have trust issues. You might always be wondering if your boyfriend or husband is cheating on you. Or if your parents left you when you were a kid, you might project that betrayal on your spouse. If you were sexually abused, that history can surface as an issue in your sex life. I encourage you to take your past to Jesus, sit down with Him, and process it. He is the only one who can make beauty out of ashes. You see, girlie, your past does not get to determine or dictate how good your future will be. With God, healing, restoration, and new beginnings are always possible.

It is also wise to take these issues to wise counsel. Reach out to community, elders at your church, and even a Christian counselor. Get as healthy as you can right now in order to be ready for the future.

I also want to encourage you that even though separations, unfaithfulness, or deaths might have happened to your parents while you were growing up, that does not mean they will happen to you in your marriage. If you did not agree with how your parents raised you, that does not mean you will be the same kind of parent. You see, your prayers make a difference. Pray for your future husband and your future marriage. Start declaring what you want to see. It is also important to remember that marriage is a commitment between three people: God, man, and woman. That means that for your marriage to succeed, the person you end up marrying must also be in a relationship with God, have similar beliefs, and be open to the Holy Spirit. You have to be going in the same direction. And do not doubt it—that is possible. Stay the course, and do not settle for less.

Ask God: Do I have any family wounds I have not healed from? How can I partner with You to bring about emotional healing?

Emotional Health: Your Appearance

It is important to be emotionally healthy regarding your appearance before starting a relationship. Living in this world makes it hard to accept yourself as you are since you are bombarded by so many examples of how women should look and what constitutes being beautiful. Some of us have had hurtful experiences with people who leave us dissatisfied with how God created us, either by a comment or a rejection. We can also go through or live around situations that bring stigma to our appearance. Take myself, for example. I was born in Honduras, but my dad's side of the family is 100 percent Arab from Bethlehem. That makes me part Arab and part Hispanic. After 9/11, I hated being associated with people from the Middle East. I associated myself with judgment from others and made myself feel less than. I had to endure going through strict security at the airport, being patted down, and sometimes even going to the "tiny room" for questioning.

I also did not like my physical appearance. I felt like my nose was too big, my legs too thick, my skin color too dark. It was not until a couple of years ago that God freed me of those mindsets. I realized I am unique and exotic. I should not be ashamed of where I come from or my ancestry. You see, I get to choose whether people's prejudices and ignorance affect me. I always have a choice.

Let's dare to take this idea even further. Girlie, God chose where you would be born and who your parents would be. He even chose how you would look. I used to hate my smile and would smile with my lips closed. After several years of getting over this, I was having a conversation with God and simply asked Him to show me what His favorite part of me was. I then forgot about the request and went out to run errands. Later that day, I went to Chipotle, where a random guy stopped me and complimented my smile. What's my point? God created you. Sometimes what we hate about ourselves is what God takes the most pride in. Be encouraged—He made you beautiful. The Bible says we are fearfully and wonderfully made. Look with me at Psalm 139 to see how David expressed this.

> For you created my inmost being;
>   you knit me together in my mother's womb.
> I praise you because I am fearfully and wonderfully made;
>   your works are wonderful,
>   I know that full well.
> My frame was not hidden from you
>   when I was made in the secret place,
>   when I was woven together in the depths of the earth.[2]
> Your eyes saw my unformed body;
>   all the days ordained for me were written in your book
>   before one of them came to be.
>
> —Ps. 139:13–16

Ask God: Are there any parts of me I am not accepting? How can I love myself better? God, show me how *You* see me.

---

2. In the Amplified Bible, Psalm 139:15 says, "And intricately *and* skillfully formed [as if embroidered with many colors] in the depths of the earth."

Emotional Health: Your Personality and Character

I also had a hard time accepting my personality. I know God gave me my attributes and way of being, but my upbringing and experiences also shaped me into who I am today. I remember always hating that I was not easy to talk to or socialize with. I hated that I was shy and introverted. I hated that I overanalyzed everything. I kept thinking, why can't I be the fun one? I wanted to be spontaneous instead of planning everything. But then I found Isaiah 45.

> *Woe to those who quarrel with their Maker,*
> *those who are nothing but potsherds*
> *among the potsherds on the ground.*
> *Does the clay say to the potter,*
> *"What are you making?"*
> *Does your work say,*
> *"The potter has no hands"?*
> *Woe to the one who says to a father,*
> *"What have you begotten?"*
> *or to a mother,*
> *"What have you brought to birth?"*
>
> —Isa. 45:9–10

If God orchestrated and directed my creation, then who am I to argue with Him? I was meant to be structured, a planner. One day, someone is going to need those attributes God has given me. Imagine if everyone was unstructured, spontaneous, and went with the flow. We would not get anything done in this world.

It is not our place to ask God why He made us a certain way. Don't get me wrong, I do not use this as an excuse to stay the same. I have learned to be intentional about not being afraid of people, about speaking up, and about being bold in God's truth. If the behaviors you have are not healthy and are not aligning with the Word of God, I encourage you to dig into His Word and find verses that speak what you want to see in your life. His Word is alive and active. Let Him transform you so you can become a testimony of His goodness and power.

A couple of years ago when I was struggling with insecurities again, God gave me a word through an acquaintance. She said, "You have asked God why He made you the way you are, but your transformation will bring glory to Him in the end." Girlie, He knows you so intimately and has already made your story beautiful. He knows what you don't like about yourself. For me, that was being too shy based on feeling less than and insecure.

When I was a kid, I was so shy that I was afraid to do anything that would make me the center of attention, even to the point of telling my teacher I had to use the restroom. Then, as an adult, I was afraid to pray in public and say the name of Jesus. You see, I feared people more than I feared God. That fear does not align with the Word of God. I let that fear and insecurity be an invitation to partner with Him, stand on His Word, and be transformed. I have definitely come a long way, but one thing I have learned is that the end result is not the prize. The prize is going through the process with God and letting Him into the deepest parts of your soul. Be open to the process—it's where the magic happens.

Ask God: What areas of my personality and character am I not fully embracing? Show me how to love the attributes You have given me, and give me discernment to know when certain behaviors are not from You.

Emotional Health: In the Waiting

What if you are already comfortable in your own skin and have accepted your beauty? That's great, but now ask yourself, "How is my emotional health in regard to the waiting season?" Are you waiting well and with purpose, or are you waiting passively while trying to get every guy's attention? It's only human to get lonely and desire relationships with others, but the way you try to find connection reveals your motives. Are you going to a friend and sharing with her? Or are you entertaining a random guy's text messages even though you know he doesn't want anything serious? Are you accepting any date offer even though you already know you are not interested? Girlie, you would not like it if a guy were wasting your time by taking you out without being intentional, so why would you do the same thing? Instead, reach out to a friend and make plans to have coffee or get together and talk about how you're feeling. God has placed friends in our lives so we can encourage one another.

The waiting season is not the time to go out with any guy just because you're bored. It is also not the time to make out with every guy you think is cute. And it is definitely not the time to compromise your purity to gain experience or fulfill your physical desires. Girlie, God has ordained this time so you can grow closer to Him, find and value yourself, and start the road toward your calling. Stop trying to get every guy's attention or every guy to like you only to get frustrated when one of them doesn't pursue you. It is not your job to find a man but to become the woman God has called you to be and to be in a position to be found. What does that look like?

- Cultivate your relationship and get to know the man Jesus by worshiping Him, reading the Word, and making Him the center of your life.
- Be plugged in, and serve in a local church. Sowing your time into others is important. Your marriage will only be as good as your selflessness.
- Be in community, those people who correct you lovingly and see the best in you.
- Start discovering your calling. What are you passionate about?
- Study toward a degree.
- Get a stable job.
- Work toward paying off any debt you have.
- Take care of your emotional and physical health.

Ask yourself: What are some practical steps I can take today to wait well?

Emotional Health: Healing from Past Relationships

If you are reading this book, it is likely you have dated or been in a relationship with someone and it did not work out. The dating process and being in a relationship are messy, vulnerable, and sometimes hurtful. I have never been in a relationship, but I did date a guy briefly that I liked. We had the same beliefs, we shared friends, and he was attractive and funny. I felt like he was such a gift from God who I did not want to lose, so I overanalyzed my every move instead of being myself. On top of that, I was shy and insecure, which did not help the process. We had very different cultures, senses of humor, and personalities. Yes, he checked most of my boxes, but I was unsure when I was with him. I felt like I had to be "on" since he might change his mind about me. I felt like I had to prove I was good enough. Needless to say, it was not effortless.

Deep down, I knew I was worth pursuing. I knew I was valuable. I knew I deserved better than what I was feeling (and what he was feeling, too), but I believed a lie. I thought the chance of another guy liking me who had his qualities was slim, so I kept trying. After feeling confused for a while, I asked for clarity, and we ended up agreeing to just be friends. Looking back, I can see how I was not ready for a relationship. I had the wrong mindset, I was not fully accepting, and I was not being myself.

I thank God for the experience, though. You might be asking, "What? You thank God for closing the opportunity to be with a guy you really liked?" The answer is yes. I've learned that what God has for me no man can take away. I've learned that when God closes one door, He is not punishing me but merely redirecting me. I've learned that when God takes something away from me, it is not to hurt me but to grow me. I've learned that one man's *no* does not determine my worth, my value, or my identity. It actually makes me run to the feet of Jesus where He speaks truth over me. You see, I've learned to trust God even when it does not make sense, because, girlie, God will never take something away from us if He does not have something better.

I wonder how many of us have been in situations like this, how many have kept pressing on the closed door just because it seemed like a good thing. How many of us have settled since we doubted that God's manifested promises over our lives were that good? How many of us stay in relationships because society says we are getting too old and all our friends are getting married? Everyone's walk is different. You are not supposed to be living up to the standards that your friends, society, or your family are putting on you. You are supposed to align with the Holy Spirit and live up to the standards He is giving you. Focus on being obedient to Him, and at the right time, if it is His will for your life, He will do it. And I believe that if God placed the desire of marriage within you, He will honor that desire in due time.

I encourage you to process those disappointments with God. The Word tells us in Proverbs 13:12 that "hope deferred makes the heart sick." So, girlie, what are you doing with that disappointment of a failed relationship or unmet expectation? The Word tells us that "the mouth speaks what the heart is full of" (Matt. 12:34). So if you are letting hope deferred take root in your heart, it will affect not only your thinking but also your actions and perspective. Be intentional to guard your heart above all else (Prov. 4:23). Here are some pointers I have learned to implement when a relationship does not work out or when everyone else is getting what you are praying for:

1. Bless the person who is getting the blessing you desire. Yes, it's hard, but you do not want bitterness or envy to be rooted in your heart.

2. Pray for the guy's future wife instead of talking bad about him with your friends.

3. Be thankful for and faithful with what you have now. Thankfulness is the pathway to joy.

4. A disappointment does not get to tell your whole story. A season is just a season.

Girlie, there is beauty in the *mystery*. Even when you don't understand, can you praise God in it? Or are you more in love with the promise than the promise-keeper? You see, praising Him in the unknown is the best sacrifice we can give God. The Word tells us that "blessed are those who have not seen and yet have believed" (John 20:29).

I'm not saying it's easy. I'm not saying it's painless. But it makes us bear fruit. Joseph's life is a prime example of this. Joseph was one of 12 sons. He was his father's favorite, which created a lot of jealousy among his brothers. Eventually, his brothers sold him into slavery, and he ended up in Egypt. He would go on to have the opportunity to be Potiphar's overseer due to his faithfulness and hard work, but regardless of his integrity, he was placed in prison because of Potiphar's wife's false accusations. He stayed there for at least two years and remained faithful to God. Imagine! Joseph had to go through a lot of trouble and obstacles to be where God intended him to be. However, because of his faithfulness to God, he would become second in command to Potiphar and would later save Egypt from famine. When his brothers came to buy food in Egypt, Joseph responded like this:

> *You intended to harm me, but God intended it for good to accomplish what is now being done, the saving of many lives.*
>
> —Gen. 50:20

Do you see the lesson here? Every time a counterfeit has broken your heart or wounded you, God has used it for your good. I'm not saying God *caused* it, but He *used* it. Romans 8:28 says, "And we know that in all things God works for the good of those who love him, who have been called according to his purpose." Believe it or not, what was birthed in me was a more intimate and sweet relationship with Jesus. For me, this looked like coming home from work and lying at His feet on my living room floor, soaking up His goodness through worship. I found that every time I took my emotions, thoughts, and insecurities to Him, He always showed up. He saw me, He knew me, and He cared about me. But listen, I did not take my emotions and try to satisfy them with worldly things like food, social media, or another guy. The only person who can truly heal and satisfy you is Jesus. He already died for your physical and even emotional healing.

I also started writing poems to the Lord to encourage myself and talk about His goodness. I stirred myself up in God. What does that look like? It's declaring what you want to see instead of what you are feeling. I am not saying we should bottle up our feelings and never deal with them. Girlie, go through those emotions and pain with Jesus. He wants your emotions, your thoughts, and even your doubts. The key is to not stay in those emotions. Take some time to go through the emotions with Jesus, and when He has restored your strength, breathed life into you, and renewed your hope, decide you are no longer dwelling on the would'ves, could'ves, or should'ves. How can God do a new thing in your life if you are going back to the old? How can He give you beauty for ashes if you are not letting go of the ashes?

After going through this process, I learned how God can fulfill and satisfy my innermost desires. I am not saying I never think about getting married or have no desire to do so, but I am saying that God has placed such a strong sense of contentment where I am that I do not need to be in a relationship to be satisfied. Look at Psalm 63 with me. David wrote this psalm when he was in the wilderness of Judah hiding from the rebellion that his own son Absalom orchestrated against him. David was probably feeling betrayed and had to endure the rough conditions of the wilderness when he was used to living as a king. Look at these verses:

> *Because your love is better than life,*
>   *my lips will glorify you.*
> *I will praise you as long as I live,*
>   *and in your name I will lift up my hands.*
> *I will be fully satisfied as with the richest of foods;*
>   *with singing lips my mouth will praise you.*
>
> —Ps. 63:3–5

This psalm teaches us how we can go to God to fill our deepest needs and heal our deepest hurts. David came to realize that no matter what condition he was facing, God's love was enough. He knew that praising God could satisfy his emotional wounds and his fleshly desires—even hunger. David had tapped into the reality that God's love can surpass any hurt, longing, or desire. I dare to stretch this even more and ask you to consider how God can satisfy the longings you have for marriage until the right time. He has promised us that He will come when we call upon Him. Be encouraged! He is faithful even when you are not. What can be better than that?

Finally, I learned how much passion I have to encourage women in their single season. I love to speak bold truths and speak identity over them. You see, God gave me beauty for my ashes. He birthed a purpose for me out of that experience. If you are going through a heartbreak or grieving a relationship that did not work out, I encourage you to partner with the Holy Spirit to renew your mind and heart. He will give you strength in this season as you meditate on His Word. Lean on these verses:

> *Jesus replied, "I am the bread of life. Whoever comes*
> *to me will never be hungry again. Whoever believes in*
> *me will never be thirsty."*
>
> —John 6:35 NLT

For he satisfies the thirsty and fills the hungry with good things.

—Ps. 107:9 NLT

My health may fail, and my spirit may grow weak, but God remains the strength of my heart; he is mine forever.

—Ps. 73:26 NLT

Come quickly, LORD, and answer me,
    for my depression deepens.
Don't turn away from me,
    or I will die.
Let me hear of your unfailing love each morning,
    for I am trusting you.
Show me where to walk,
    for I give myself to you.

—Ps. 143:7–8 NLT

Ask God: Are there any past relationships or hurts I have not completely healed from or given to You? How can I partner with You to bring about emotional healing in this area?

Emotional Health: Forgiveness

Once you have accepted yourself and are loving yourself by God's grace, you can forgive others. The Bible says, "We love each other because he first loved us" (1 John 4:19). Forgiveness is a way of expressing love—love toward yourself and love toward others. It frees you! Most of the time, people do not have the right perspective about forgiveness. They think that when they forgive, they are agreeing that what was done to them is acceptable. That is not the case. When you forgive, you are letting go of resentment and anger. You are removing bitter roots from your heart and, instead, allowing God to dwell there and make it flourish. You might be thinking, "If I forgive this person, that means I have to pretend nothing happened and be in a relationship with them." That is not the case, either. Just because you forgive someone does not mean you have to be in a relationship with them. You are simply letting go of the chain you are keeping between you and that person. You are freeing yourself and giving that person a gift.

Jesus said in Matthew 6:14–15, "For if you forgive other people when they sin against you, your heavenly Father will also forgive you. But if you do not forgive others their sins, your Father will not forgive your sins." This is not to bring condemnation but to highlight the importance Jesus, the Son of God, placed on forgiveness. Who are we to keep a record of wrongs when we are far from perfect ourselves? Let's sow the forgiveness God has given us to other people who have hurt us. In the end, everything is from Him and unto Him.

In Luke 31, Paul adds that forgiving one another is showing kindness and compassion. Those who hurt you might not have intended to do so. Sometimes, hurt people only know how to hurt others. Girlie, be merciful to them. They may not have had a good example. That is not to make excuses for them but only to show the love of Christ and live from a renewed mind. What does that look like? Here's what the Bible tells us:

> *Finally, brothers and sisters, whatever is true, whatever is noble, whatever is right, whatever is pure, whatever is lovely, whatever is admirable—if anything is excellent or praiseworthy—think about such things.*
>
> —Phil. 4:8

Ask God: Is there someone I am harboring resentment toward that I have not forgiven? What steps do You want me to take regarding this?

Ending Prayer

If you are ready to forgive those you resent in your heart and are ready to let go of the old so God can bring something new, pray this prayer:

> LORD, *thank You for dying on the cross for me and bearing the weight of my sins. I thank You for forgiving me of all my faults and making me as white as snow. I come to you humbly, asking You to take away all resentment, pain, and bitterness in my heart toward _____. I know what they did was not right, but I choose to forgive them like You forgave me. Thank You for giving me beauty for my ashes and for meeting me where I am. I trust You. Amen.*

CHAPTER SIX

Physical Health

Physical health is one of my favorite topics since I am a registered dietitian and nutritionist. I love helping people, specifically women, find a realistic and approachable eating pattern to feel their best. As I was growing up, I had access to healthy foods, but most Hispanic cooking consists of excessive refined carbohydrates and unhealthy fats. One of my grandmothers had a restaurant, and the other one constantly baked desserts. Needless to say, I had a couple of extra pounds hanging around. It wasn't until my grandpa had to have coronary bypass surgery that my family became more health-conscious. My mom started going to several dietitians to lose weight, and I tagged along to keep her company.

I was intrigued and amazed how food could affect the body. My mom's obsession with weight soon affected me. Thankfully, I never had an eating disorder, but I did count calories and overexercise. I finally lost weight before my high school graduation and went on to study nutrition. A bachelor's degree, a master's degree, and an internship later, I became a nutrition expert. I am thankful that I do not obsess over calories anymore. Instead, eating healthy has become my normal.

Why do I share this? I don't want you to become hyperfocused on a number on the scale or how many calories you are eating per day. Instead, focus on what makes you feel good. The Bible tells us to take care of our bodies. I'm not saying that counting calories is bad, but rather the mindset you have and the power you give that number is what can make it unhealthy. If you are in the process of losing weight and a calorie tracker helps you gain perspective of what you are eating, go for it, but don't let that number dictate your happiness.

Look at 1 Corinthians 6:19–20 with me:

> *Do you not know that your bodies are temples of the Holy Spirit, who is in you, whom you have received from God? You are not your own; you were bought at a price. Therefore honor God with your bodies.*

Your body is where God the Holy Spirit resides. Be intentional about taking care of it. If you are currently eating processed and junk food every day, why not try cooking your meals at home? A calorie is not just a calorie. Try to choose healthy food options that are filled with vitamins and minerals, not just empty calories. If you don't know how to cook, invest in that. There are many in-person or online cooking classes. Or even better, why not buy a healthy cookbook and have a cooking night with your friends? These are basic skills that are good to have even down the road. If you desire marriage and eventually kids, how are you going to help them thrive if you don't have the skills to do so?

One of the easiest ways to start improving your health is eating more fruits and vegetables and decreasing the amount of refined sugars you are eating. As a rule of thumb, half of your plate should be filled with vegetables. When I say vegetables, think of those that are not starchy, such as broccoli, cauliflower, lettuce, kale, green beans, eggplant, spaghetti squash, and others. The other half of your plate should consist of complex carbohydrates and lean protein. Examples of complex carbohydrates are brown rice, quinoa, and 100 percent whole-grain spaghetti or bread. You could also use starchy veggies such as sweet potatoes, plantains, corn, or regular potatoes. The lean proteins are those with no visible fat or skin such as lean chicken, turkey, beef, and fish. If you eat ground beef, try to find 99 percent fat-free. Then you can have nuts, fruits, and dairy as snacks or even dessert. What you eat even affects your mind. Make an intentional effort to get healthy, not just from the outside but also on the inside.

Eating healthy is important, but exercise is also an essential component to feeling great and confident. Do you know that working out gives you free endorphins? They are the feel-good chemicals your nervous system produces. They help you fight pain and boost your energy levels. Exercise also helps you stay in shape, build muscle mass, and prevent chronic diseases such as obesity, high blood pressure, diabetes, and cholesterol. If you are not sure how to start, join a gym or a group class, or work out to online videos on YouTube. I don't know about you, but I have decided to live a long, healthy life serving God.

Once you have found a healthy eating and exercise routine, thank God that you are able to move and nourish your body. Accept who God has made you to be, make the most of it, and be confident in your own skin. How do you do that? Speak love and acceptance over yourself by saying, "I am fearfully and wonderfully made," "I am beautiful," "I am content with who I am." If there are parts of your body you don't like, take them to the Lord and let Him speak to you and love you in that area. It might seem silly, but He cares.

On a similar note, most guys are not attracted to just one feature. If you feel like you aren't symmetrical or aren't as beautiful as your standard of beauty, you are setting yourself up for failure. A godly man is not looking for a supermodel. He is looking for someone he can do life with and serve God with. Guys don't think, "Wow, that girl has a beautiful nose! I need to take her out for coffee." They see the whole package. They think, "Am I attracted to this girl? Is she confident? Is she smart? Can I have a conversation with her?" A godly guy understands that marriage is not just looks and sex; it is companionship, partnership, a mission, and a representation of God's love for us. Make a decision today that you are going to believe in your heart that you are beautiful, and then act like it. Confidence is key!

While we are being honest, most men *are* attracted to physical beauty first. I am not saying a man can't like you for your inner beauty, but most guys approach you because they think you are beautiful or because they are attracted to you in some way. That does not mean you have to wear seductive clothing, wear tons of makeup, and try to get every guy's attention. But it does mean you have to be intentional about how you present yourself when you go out. Are you brushing your teeth and fixing your hair? Are you removing unwanted hair from your face (eyebrows, lips)? Are you wearing matching and decent clothing? Are you taking care of your skin? There's nothing wrong with investing in a good facial once in a while. Girlie, if you are not taking care of and loving yourself, how will you take care of and love someone else well?

If you wear makeup, then wear makeup, and own it. Makeup is not a sin. The motives behind why you use it are what matters. Are you doing it as a fun, girly thing that relieves stress and gives you a little confidence boost? That's fine. If you use makeup to gain all your confidence or seek attention, maybe you need to do a heart check: "Why am I not confident without makeup? Is all my identity there?" You see, making yourself look presentable from the outside is not a bad thing as long as you are also pouring into your character and checking your motives. And if you don't wear makeup, I am not saying you have to start using it. If you feel confident in your own skin without having to touch up, more power to you.

Let's take Ruth's story in the Bible as an example. As you may know, Ruth was a Moabite married to one of Naomi's sons. In Moab, Naomi's husband and sons died, so she headed to Bethlehem with her daughter-in-law, Ruth. There, Ruth was able to marry Boaz, her kinsman redeemer. But how did she get there? Besides being faithful to Naomi and being a servant, she presented herself well.

Wash, put on perfume, and get dressed in your best clothes. Then go down to the threshing floor, but don't let him know you are there until he has finished eating and drinking.

—Ruth 3:3

Naomi did not tell Ruth to go see Boaz after she worked in the fields all day. She knew that taking care of her body and presenting it well mattered. Another example is Queen Esther. Before she became royalty, she lived with her cousin in Susa, where the king was looking for another queen. Esther qualified as a contender since she was a beautiful virgin. She was taken into the palace along with all the other women to get ready to be presented to the king. To be able to be in the king's presence, she had to complete 12 months of beauty treatments. Imagine that!

In addition to taking care of their appearance, these two women took the advice of well-seasoned role models. Both Ruth and Esther listened to those who knew the ground well. Ruth followed Naomi's plan to a T and ended up marrying Boaz. Esther accepted the advice of Hegai, the eunuch in charge of the harems, and was made queen. With Hegai's help and God's grace, Esther stood out from the crowd. The Bible says, "She [Esther] asked for nothing other than what Hegai, the king's eunuch who was in charge of the harem, suggested. And Esther won the favor of everyone who saw her" (Esther 2:15). But what if Esther had started comparing herself to the other women around her and asked for the extra accessories, makeup, and fragrances they were using? She would have stepped outside her lane.

There are several lessons here. First, listening to wise counsel is an important step in getting where you want to in life, whether that is being a fulfilled single person or eventually being married. Second, instead of trying to look like another woman, embrace your beauty. We do not need two of the same person. We need you to be you and run your own race. Finally, sometimes less is more. You don't have to wear a ton of makeup, huge accessories, a wild hairstyle, and a provocative outfit to get men's attention. You definitely will find attention, but it won't result in what you desire—someone to value you and treat you with standards. Girlie, the man God has for you will love your outward appearance, but when he gets to know your heart, he will discover the gold. Outward appearance is just a door opener, but the real surprise is inside your heart. Remember, take care of your body, but also invest in your inner beauty.

Ending Prayer

Father, I recognize that this body is Yours and that it is a temple of the Holy Spirit. I pray that You would give me the self-control to choose how to healthfully nourish Your temple. Thank You, Lord, for giving me the strength and wisdom to take care of Your body so I have the strength to glorify You on earth. Amen.

CHAPTER SEVEN

Finding Your Identity and Calling

Identity. That's who you are and what makes you different from everyone else. Identity was always very special to me. For most of my life, I did not know my identity. I focused most of my life on being a good daughter and student, and therefore my identity was deeply rooted in performance. It showed up in how many As, diplomas, and recognitions I got. I didn't really make time in my high school or college years to find what I was good at since I was focused on studying, getting a scholarship, and being an A student. After finishing all my studies, I was feeling empty. Where was I going to get my worth from now that school was over? There were no more tests to pass or scholarships to get. I had no books to hide behind anymore. I no longer had an A to strive for as my identity.

I became eager to find out who I was and decided to try a lot of things to figure out what I liked and what I was good at. I got plugged in to a church of Levites whose mission was ministering to the Lord, and most people there either played an instrument or sang. I decided to learn to play the piano. I got a used keyboard and asked a friend to teach me. But the piano wasn't for me, and I gave up after one week. I tried teaching toddlers about Jesus in Sunday school, but I needed someone to talk back to me. I tried taking care of flowers, but

I killed even a succulent. I tried learning calligraphy, but after the class, I never touched the pen. I also served as a greeter and cleaner at church, but even though I liked serving, I knew I had more in me. I tried being a sweet encourager like one of my friends, and that was not me. You see, I was trying to be someone else instead of asking God who I was. The only thing I did consistently for two years was disciple a girl who was a new believer, but I still did not see the big picture.

Eventually, a woman at church gave me a prophetic word. She said, "You've made God the center of your life, and because of that, He'll show you your identity and take you wherever you want. Your face will shine with the countenance of the glory of the Lord." I was ecstatic. I began spending many nights asking God, "Why did you make me?" One day I woke up, and as I did, I sensed God downloading one of my passions: ministering to women. I have finally reached the other side and can say I know part but not all of my identity since God reveals in parts.

First and foremost, I am a daughter of the Most High and was bought with a high price. I am royalty but also a servant of God. I am a child of God who was made to speak truth boldly in love and who thrives in encouraging and challenging women to live a life of faith, purpose, and purity. I am also a light in dark places and delight in praying for other people.

With all this revelation came opportunities to serve God. You see, if you do not have your identity deeply rooted in Jesus and what He says about you, you are fickle and wavering. Any comment will shake you. Once my identity was set on a steady rock, I started an Instagram page to encourage and challenge women (@living_setapart), I wrote this book, I applied to be part of the prophetic ministry at church, and I was asked to help with prayer sets. All this did not happen immediately. God's promise over my identity was in 2017, and I am just barely starting to see the fruit of that word.

I am in a season where I *know* my worth and value is in Jesus and not in my performance. I am in a season where I *know* Jesus, so I am not afraid to step out or to fail. I am in a season where I do not base my actions on a fear of people. I have learned that when you develop a fear of God, the fear of people diminishes. If God is proud, I am satisfied. I was not created to please people but to serve and please God.

If you are not sure who you are as a person, ask God to show you. He created you. He knit you together in your mother's womb with likes, dislikes, things you are good at, and a unique personality. So how do you find who you really are? First, ask God to reveal your identity to you. Then go to His Word, the Bible, and declare those truths over yourself. Ephesians is a great book to start in. Once you have that steady foundation, start trying new things. See where your heart comes alive and what makes it fire up.

While you do this, don't get jealous of the gifts and qualities other people have. Instead, celebrate those gifts. God has enough gifts, talents, and anointing for everyone. Girlie, we don't need you to be like your friend. We need you to be *you*. We need you to express God in *your* unique way. That is why God *created, chose,* and *handpicked* you to be here on earth. He is intentional with what He created. I also encourage you to check the fears within you. For example, all my life I dealt with insecurity that showed up as a fear of people, a fear of praying in public, and a fear of being too vulnerable. Now I see that all those fears were tactics of the enemy to try to blind me to what God has planned for me to do. Being vulnerable, bold, and prayerful are all attributes I need for my calling.

Look at 1 Corinthians 12 where Paul talks about how we (the church) are one body with different parts that are essential for it to thrive. If you want to be like someone else, we would be missing the essential part of what you have to offer.

If the whole body were an eye, where would the sense of hearing be? If the whole body were an ear, where would the sense of smell be? But in fact God has placed the parts in the body, every one of them, just as he wanted them to be. If they were all one part, where would the body be?

—1 Cor. 12:17–19

It is also important to know that your identity does not come from your marital status, your position, your socioeconomic status, or what others say about you. Jesus is where you find your identity. But how can you know if you are placing your identity in something other than Jesus? Girlie, search your heart, partner with the Holy Spirit, and ask yourself, "Am I getting my worth from something or someone other than Jesus?" God only reveals to heal you, not condemn you.

If you are being shaken by a guy's rejection, you are placing your worth and value in a guy's opinion of you. Being rejected does not determine your identity. Sometimes, man's rejection is God's redirection. Just because a guy does not find you attractive or does not ask you out does not mean you are worthless. You do not have to be liked by every guy. Your worth and value come from above. Stop asking yourself what is wrong with you. If a guy did not pursue you well and was not intentional, he was just not interested in marrying you. And that's okay. Is it not better to know that now and avoid marrying the wrong person? As long as you are walking in obedience and surrender, what God has for you will end up being yours. Stop thinking that you missed your chance due to past mistakes or mindsets. You are not more powerful than Almighty God.

Your identity also does not come from your looks, your position, what you do, or how many likes you get on social media. You are a daughter of God who was made with a purpose—to make God

known. I pray that you will tap into the revelation of His love for you.
Speak and declare His truth over your life. Here are some examples
of declarations to pour into your spirit:

- I am beautifully and wonderfully made (Ps. 139:14).
- I am deeply rooted in God's love (Eph. 3:17).
- I am God's favorite (Ps. 30:7 MSG).
- I am worthy of pursuit (Eph. 5:25).
- I hear God's voice easily (John 10:27).
- I am lavishly loved by Jesus (Rom. 5:8).
- I am full of joy and peace (John 14:27).
- I shift atmospheres with my faith (Matt. 17:20).
- I bring clarity to confusing situations (James 1:5).
- I have the mind of Christ (1 Cor. 2:16).
- I am impactful and full of wisdom (James 1:5).
- I do not live by my feelings but by the Spirit (Prov. 29:11).
- I walk in holiness and purity (1 Pet. 1:15–16, Ps. 24:3–4).
- No mistake is too big for God's love (Ps. 25:7, Heb. 8:12).
- I do not settle for less than what God has ordained for me (Isa. 55:2).
- I bring light to the dark places, and I expose darkness (Eph. 5:8–13).
- I am quick to listen, slow to speak, and slow to become angry (James 1:19).
- I am more than a conqueror through Christ who strengthens me (Rom. 8:37).
- I do not live by bread alone but by every word of the living God (Matt. 4:4).
- I was made to fulfill a significant assignment on this earth (Jer. 1:5, 29:11).
- I have chosen the greater thing and do not submit to lesser lovers (Luke 10:42).
- I am a chosen people, a royal priesthood, a holy nation, God's special possession (1 Pet. 2:9).

- I do not compare myself with other women, but I love them and empower them (Gal. 5:26, 6:4–6).
- I do not conform to the patterns of this world, but I am transformed by the renewing of my mind (Rom. 12:2).
- I have been chosen and appointed for extraordinary things (1 Pet. 2:9, Jer. 1:5, Eph. 3:20).
- Other people's rejections do not dictate my value. I am a child of God, and I am loved and accepted by the one true king (Eph. 1:3–6).

Purpose versus Calling

I believe God placed us on earth to have fellowship with Him. He created Adam and Eve to spend time with Him in the garden. God actually walked in the garden with them. That relationship also applies to us, but we have an even better companion. When Jesus left earth, He left us the Holy Spirit to live in our hearts. What greater intimacy and companionship is there? I also believe God created us to make Him known.

> *Then Jesus came to them and said, "All authority in heaven and on earth has been given to me. Therefore go and make disciples of all nations, baptizing them in the name of the Father and of the Son and of the Holy Spirit, and teaching them to obey everything I have commanded you. And surely I am with you always, to the very end of the age."*
>
> —Matt. 28:18–20

When Jesus ascended to heaven, He told His disciples to go and make disciples and teach them His ways. Girlie, God made you to shine your light brightly. You might be asking, "Well, how do I do that?" We make Him known through our calling. I currently work as a dietitian with kids who have developmental disabilities. You can imagine the families and situations I witness every day, but I know God has placed me there to love and encourage those families. While I was trying to figure out who I was, I prayed for the families I work with. I loved them well. I spoke truth over them.

Remember, your calling is where you are *now* and with the people God has placed around you. Sometimes, we get so fixated on arriving, getting a platform, and being well-known that we forsake the season we are in now. But if God can't trust you with a little, how can He trust you with much? Your calling now might look like being a preacher. For others, your calling could be encouraging someone at work, praying for people, leading a Bible study, or equipping the church. For me, it looks like being a light in dark and hopeless places by praying for and encouraging my patients and their families. It's encouraging girls and reminding them of their value and purpose. If you are ready to know how God wants you to do this, ask Him to start revealing His calling for your life. The Bible says He has planted a sense of purpose in our lives.

> He has also planted eternity [a sense of divine purpose] in the human heart [a mysterious longing which nothing under the sun can satisfy, except God]—yet man cannot find out (comprehend, grasp) what God has done (His overall plan) from the beginning to the end.
>
> —Eccles. 3:11 AMP

Whatever you are good at is usually how God has wired you to spread His Good News, whether as a fitness instructor who motivates girls or a teacher who prays and speaks truth over her kids. Either way, you are shining your light brightly. Consider Ephesians 4:1–3 where Paul challenges us to live a life worthy of the calling God has placed in us:

As a prisoner for the LORD, then, I urge you to live a life worthy of the calling you have received. Be completely humble and gentle; be patient, bearing with one another in love. Make every effort to keep the unity of the Spirit through the bond of peace.

I don't know about you, but I want to completely fulfill what God has planned for me. I want God to be proud of me and tell me, "Well done, good and faithful servant!" as I finish my journey on this earth. I don't want to waste the opportunities He gives me. I want to please Him. You see, I believe there is nothing more we can do or any mistake we can make that will make God love us more or less, but I do think we ought to make an effort to please Him.

Don't Compromise Your Purpose and Calling

Let's go to the story of Esau and Jacob, the sons of Rebekah and Isaac. Esau was the firstborn, so he had the birthright, an honor given to firstborns at that time. It implied that they would possess a double portion of the family's material goods and eventually become the family's leader. As Esau grew older, he became a skilled hunter. On the other hand, Jacob preferred to stay at home. One day, Esau came back from hunting and was starving. He saw that Jacob was making some stew, so he asked for some. Jacob, seeing that Esau was desperate, asked Esau to trade his birthright for the stew, and Esau swore that he would.

You might be asking, "Janelle, what does this have to do with my walk with God?" This story depicts how sometimes we compromise God's best for our lives to meet our fleshly desires. Esau's fleshly desire was that he was feeling very hungry. But for us single ladies, how many times do we feel like compromising just to have someone to hold hands with or someone to take home for the holidays? Let me take it a little further. How many of us have compromised our purity for a bowl of stew? Girlie, it is not worth it. And just because all your friends are dating and everyone is getting married does not mean it is the right time for you. Do your part to stand firm in your standards and values, and know your worth.

Marriage is your second-most important decision after accepting Jesus as your Lord and Savior. When God puts man and woman together, the focus is on *purpose*. God has a plan for them to serve Him and make Him known. Why compromise the plan God has already ordained for your marriage or for your future generations? Your obedience today will affect others later on. When you are tempted to settle, pause and look for perspective. Will you give in to short-term satisfaction, or will you practice self-control and delayed gratification? Don't let your feelings control you. Even though your feelings are real, you get to decide how you act. Remember, God chose you, knitted you together, and placed you on this earth with a mission. Will you patiently wait for God to provide while you fulfill your mission?

God's Timing for the Activation of Your Calling

Don't get discouraged if what God tells you does not happen quickly. Most of the time, God is just planting the seed, and it has to grow and mature. It will come to pass in due season if you continue to lean on Him, follow His Spirit, and obey Him. I got the word of my identity in 2017, and I am just starting to see it come to pass. I went through two years of being intentional with God, letting Him mold me and being obedient to Him. Don't expect a microwavable promise when God is into slow cookers. Consider David. He knew God had called him to be king, but it took time for him to see the promise come to pass. At the time he wrote Psalm 57, he was being persecuted by King Saul. Did David complain, lose hope, or give up? No. David was confident that God would work out His plan for his life.

> *I cry out to God Most High,*
> *to God who fulfills his purpose for me.*
> —Ps. 57:2 ESV

God usually speaks to the spiritual realm before He manifests the promises in the natural realm. God told David he would be king, but David waited several years before he actually sat on the throne. Why does God do that? Because He uses that waiting season to mold and prepare us for the promise, and in the waiting period, He wants us to use His spoken promises over us as an anchor to continue pressing on. Girlie, I encourage you to fill your mind and soul with verses of God's faithfulness. Here are some of those key verses:

> The LORD will fulfill his purpose for me;
> your steadfast love, O LORD, endures forever.
> Do not forsake the work of your hands.
> —Ps. 138:8 ESV

> And I am sure of this, that he who began a good work in you will bring it to completion at the day of Jesus Christ.
> —Phil. 1:6 ESV

> For we are his workmanship, created in Christ Jesus for good works, which God prepared beforehand, that we should walk in them.
> —Eph. 2:10 ESV

I also encourage you to keep God out of the box of how you believe things will happen and what you think He has for you. God's ways are not our ways. He can use anything you give Him and turn it into something beautiful. Believe it or not, I was a shy, introverted girl with low self-esteem. I knew about God but did not know Him intimately. I was so shy that I was even scared to pray out loud and say the name of Jesus. My least favorite subject was English, and I especially hated writing. I also did not think I was creative. Who would have thought that God had placed a passion inside me to teach women their worth and value through social media or to write a book about how to live set apart during singleness? But that is how God works—in mysterious and unusual ways.

Don't Hold Back When He Reveals Your Calling to You

Once you've found the passion God has placed in your heart, be obedient to it. Sometimes, we get caught up in what the world thinks: "If I actually do this, will I be too weird?" or "There are already too many people doing the same thing." What He placed in you is significant. Do not think lightly of it. There are some people only *you* can reach with your vision. Be obedient to God's call. When we stand before God, we will not be judged according to what we did but according to what we were *called* to do and whether we did it. Look at the following verses:

> *So we make it our goal to please him, whether we are at home in the body or away from it. For we must all appear before the judgment seat of Christ, so that each of us may receive what is due us for the things done while in the body, whether good or bad.*
> —2 Cor. 5:9–10

> *Watch yourselves, so that you do not lose what we have accomplished together, but that you may receive a full and perfect reward [when He grants rewards to faithful believers].*
> —2 John 1:8 AMP

Endure the race and get the full reward. God has already planned what you are meant to do and has placed that desire in your heart. Do not get carried away in this world and start going through the motions. I know it's hard to step out, but do not stop dreaming with

Him. Do not get numb to His plans. Do not get too comfortable where you are that you forget to live out your mission. I encourage you to seek God's face to get a revelation of His will for your life. No matter what He has called you to do, be the best at it and remember that obedience pleases God more than sacrifice.

God is so purposeful that He intentionally placed a specific calling and purpose in you and in your future husband separately. But when you come together, it will multiply and expand. Girlie, when your husband's and your life's purpose and vision come together, you will be able to impact and reach more people for God's glory. My prayer is that you will desire purpose more than butterflies. You see, butterflies are fleeting, but purpose is long-lasting and impacts other people and generations. It is meaningful.

Ending Prayer

Father, I thank You for breathing purpose into me even before I was born. Your Word says that Your plans for me are good, and I believe it. I pray that You will reveal to me what You have created me to accomplish on this earth for You. I do not want to miss it. Thank You for giving me the boldness and strength to do it. I bind any fear of people and declare that I have only fear of You, Lord. I trust You. Amen.

CHAPTER EIGHT

Purity

Once you feel that you have healed emotionally, have a sense of purpose, and have a vision of where God is taking you, be open to dating or courtship. But before you do that, it's important to have already processed with Jesus the concept of celibacy. That might seem drastic, but if you have not made up your mind about where you stand on physical touch boundaries, it will be easier to compromise your purity once you are tempted. Take a look at the definitions below from the *Cambridge Dictionary*.

> purity (n): the state of not being mixed with anything else
> abstinence (n): the act of not doing something, especially something that gives you pleasure
> celibate (adj): not having sex, especially because you have made a religious promise not to

Yes, we've all heard the terms *purity, abstinence,* and *celibacy,* but do we know what they really mean? When we make it our effort to be pure in this world, we are deciding not to mix with what it offers so we can be free of contamination. What does that look like? Guarding your heart. The Bible tells us, "Above all else, guard your heart, for everything you do flows from it" (Prov. 4:23). Whatever you are feeding your heart will come out as thoughts and actions. If you are watching sexual shows or pornography or listening to explicit music, how do you expect to have pure thoughts? The only basis for engaging in those things is lust. I challenge you to start removing those pollutants from your life and replace them with worship music, sermons, and the Word of God. If you want to reap purity, you have to sow pure content in your heart. Out of that, complete satisfaction in Jesus will reap a desire to be celibate *for Him*. And yes, I know celibacy gets a bad reputation since most people think it only applies to priests and nuns, but the truth is that you can be celibate for a season and then get married. Abstinence is merely withholding from any sexual activity for any reason, while celibacy is doing it with a heart posture to please God.

I grew up in a Hispanic household, so being abstinent was a big deal. When I was growing up, I knew that having sex before marriage was a big no-no, and because there was a lot of fear and shame associated with sex, I avoided it. As a result, I was abstaining simply because that's what you did—it was a religious spirit and a cultural norm. Even writing this section was challenging because it did not flow like the others. I asked God why, and He said, "Because you are not living it." I was shocked, but I knew God was referring to my heart since I've never been in a relationship with a guy. He said, "You know the legalism behind abstinence, but you have not tapped into My heart for it." Wow! I knew what He meant. I was walking in the religious spirit of being abstinent instead of knowing what God has to say about it.

Now that I *know* God intimately, I have a deeper revelation of His intent for guarding sex for marriage. I have decided to live in celibacy for Him until I meet my husband and we make a covenant. You see, God created sex, and it is good. It is nothing to be ashamed of. God's plan of intimacy started when He made Eve specifically for Adam, and the Bible says they were united into *one*. Matthew 19:6 says, "So they [husband and wife] are no longer two, but one flesh. Therefore what God has joined together, let no one separate." When the Bible mentions "united into one" or "one flesh," it means that men and women became one both emotionally and physically. It is a special and powerful act, which is why God wants to *protect* you from having this experience with multiple people.

God wants you to experience sex at the right time and with the right person. He is not a God who withholds good things (Ps. 84:11), but He is a God who has a season and a time for everything (Eccles. 3:11). Trust Him! Just because it is not happening now does not mean it will not happen further down the road. It is like a child trying to drive a car, and his parents keep telling him he is too young but that his time will come. If his parents allowed him to drive, he would probably get in a wreck and hurt himself and others. The same thing happens when you engage in sexual activities and sex before marriage. Your partner and you will be hurt since you are sharing an intimate experience that you were created to share with only one person.

In the Song of Solomon, King Solomon warns us not to awaken love before it's your time.

> *Daughters of Jerusalem, I charge you:*
> *Do not arouse or awaken love*
> *until it so desires.*

—Song of Songs 8:4

What does that look like? Dating before you are ready to commit to marriage, having sex before marriage, or even having emotional and deep conversations with a man who is not in a relationship with you. Paul talks about purity in Ephesians 5 and 1 Thessalonians 4 where he was addressing two churches. He challenges us to be free of any sexual immorality and impurity by learning to *control* our bodies. Look at the following verses:

But among you there must not be even a hint of sexual immorality, or of any kind of impurity, or of greed, because these are improper for God's holy people. Nor should there be obscenity, foolish talk or coarse joking, which are out of place, but rather thanksgiving. For of this you can be sure: No immoral, impure or greedy person—such a person is an idolater—has any inheritance in the kingdom of Christ and of God.

—Eph. 5:3–5

It is God's will that you should be sanctified: that you should avoid sexual immorality; that each of you should learn to control your own body in a way that is holy and honorable.

—1 Thess. 4:3–4

Ouch! Why do you think Paul was so cautious and stern about this? First, Paul understood that sexual sin is not only sinning against God but also against your *own body* (1 Cor. 6:18). Do I dare take it further and suggest that we would be sinning against our future husband as well? Second, Paul understood that what God created was something special *and* powerful. Sex creates an emotional bond. During sex, you release a hormone called oxytocin, which is one of the hormones that make you feel happy. That hormone also increases the feelings of trust and intimacy toward your partner. I don't know about you, but I do not want to feel like that for anyone except the person God has for me.

Engaging in sex can also leave a lot of wounds that will have to be healed before you meet your husband. When you have sex, you are engaging your spirit, soul, and body, causing something called a soul tie when part of your partner stays with you from then on, whether that connection is good or bad. Girlie, do not lengthen the healing process you will have to go through, but instead, lean on God for strength and wisdom. A guy who cares about you would not want to take you to the altar with a blemish. He would respect, honor, and want the best for you. I know some of you might be asking, "What about everything else besides sex?" If you have to ask if something is allowed, then it's probably too far. Look at what the Bible says.

> *Be devoted to one another in love. Honor one another*
> *above yourselves.*
> —Rom. 12:10

> *Treat younger men as brothers, older women as mothers,*
> *and younger women as sisters, with absolute purity.*
> —1 Tim. 5:1–2

The Bible does not have a dating instruction manual since dating did not exist in Bible times. The only thing God tells us is to love and respect one another as brothers and sisters. What does that look like? Well, do not do anything you would not do to your brother. During the dating season, you are just supposed to be getting to know someone. Ask yourself these questions: "Do I like being around him? Can I keep a conversation with him? Does he have similar beliefs?" If you can't even hold a conversation and have no common ground, what makes you think a marriage relationship will succeed? Sex is merely one part of marriage. Talking, sharing, and doing life together make up a much greater part. Do not let physical touch and crossing boundaries mess with your judgment and evaluation process during the dating season.

I dare you to take this deeper than just sex. Why not live purely for God in every area? Instead of deciding to leave sex only for marriage, why not abstain from all the things that can lead to sex? Sex starts with your mind. Are you letting your thoughts go wild about a guy you think is hot? Are you being lustful when you see an attractive man? Are you letting guys make out with you and feel your body? Are you masturbating or looking at pornography? I know we are already pure in God's eyes because of Christ's sacrifice, but that does not mean we should live without putting in any effort. The Bible says, "Blessed are the pure in heart, for they will see God (Matt. 5:8). The purity that you practice during your single season *will* reap a harvest during your marriage because you will have mastered the self-control you need in marriage. You will also not have to deal with thoughts about you and your exes.

If you are no longer a virgin, if you have been engaging in sexual activities and have not been guarding your purity, you can still make the commitment today. God is a God of love, mercy, and second chances. His love is strong. It is mighty. It is relentless toward you. It does not back down when things get tough. It doesn't leave when you make a mistake. Instead, it presses in. It holds tight. It does not let you go. So if you are ready to commit and want to live for God alone by guarding your innocence, body, and heart, repeat this prayer with me:

> *God, thank You for loving me unconditionally. Forgive me for sinning against You and my body and for not living up to my worth and value. I am done living life my way and compromising my purity. I make a choice to live for You starting today. Give me strength to live a holy life, and give me the wisdom to discern right from wrong. I give You all the experiences and thoughts I have from past relationships that have not pleased You. Thank You for restoring my purity and making me as white as snow. I want to be completely Yours before I am a man's. Draw me close. Pursue me. I love you.*

If you prayed that prayer, then believe that your purity has been restored. Rejoice! Guarding your purity may not be easy, but I am confident that with God by your side, you will have the strength. You can do it. You should also begin thinking about choosing your friends wisely. Some people will judge you and say you are boring and old-fashioned for choosing purity. But often that criticism comes from people who aren't in a relationship with Jesus or who just feel badly about themselves and want you to feel the same way.

The Bible says that "your enemy the devil prowls around like a roaring lion looking for someone to devour" (1 Pet. 5:8). What does that mean? It means you need to have a strategy to protect your purity. Here are some key strategies:

1. Surround yourself with like-minded Christian women who can support you in this season.
2. Have an accountability partner, and share your struggles with her.
3. Be careful about what TV shows, movies, and images you are watching, as well as what music you are listening to.
4. Set your physical boundaries before you meet someone. You know what tempts you the most.
5. Be mindful of your thoughts, and don't allow them to go wherever they want. You are in control of them.

Although staying celibate for God is an awesome thing, I want to make something clear. The end goal of abstaining from sexual sin is not to get a pat on the back because you can follow a rule. It is not to be able to fit the Christian label. It is also not to feel superior to others or to get a prize. Girlie, the actual prize is finding how only the man Jesus can satisfy you, even in your carnal desires. I know that may be hard to grasp, but He is the *only* source of living water. The Bible tells us that "whoever drinks the water I [Jesus] give them will never thirst" (John 4:14). You see, once you marry this man Jesus by inviting Him into your life, saying "I do" and making a covenant with Him, you ought to look to Him to satisfy. Out of this relationship, you will have the strength to exercise self-control, which is a fruit of the Spirit.

Girlie, when you drink from the real fountain of life and the real, satiating living water, you no longer thirst for the insatiable and temporary waters of lesser lovers. Finally, Jesus tells us, "Indeed, the water I give them will become in them a spring of water welling up to eternal life" (John 4:14). What does that mean? When Jesus gives you the Holy Spirit, the eternal living water, He resides in you and makes a spring that is ever-feeding you satiating water. Isn't that amazing? So, girlie, when you feel thirsty for those lesser lovers, ask the Holy Spirit to quench your thirst. He is right there with you.

CHAPTER NINE

Marriage

What Is Marriage?

We finally got to marriage! If you chose this book, I am assuming you desire to get married. And that is awesome! Longing to get married is not bad, and you should not be ashamed to speak your heart. Jesus placed that desire in you, but you have to assess what you are actually desiring. You see, sometimes we idolize the idea of marriage, yet we have not tapped into what being a wife or making a covenant is. If you are viewing marriage as an idol, you will be disappointed. When we idolize something, we give it a higher value than God and therefore place all our hope and expectations in something other than Him. A man will never be able to satisfy all the longings of your soul—only God can. God is the One who is perfect and has no blemish. Men are human and therefore prone to make mistakes.

Of course, marriage is an amazing blessing from God. But I want to give you the facts and prepare your heart for marriage since often we see marriage only as a Disney fairy-tale story. I want you to see the side that is not commonly talked about in the happily-ever-afters. Marriage is not a way to graduate from singleness. Yes, it is an incredible thing to be able to share your life with someone you love, but know that marriage is putting someone else's needs and desires above yours. It is not being spoiled and served all the time. It is a covenant relationship in which you learn to die daily to make your relationship thrive. It's saying yes to a person every day, even if you do not feel attracted to them sometimes or don't agree with their opinion. Marriage and love are a choice. Of course, you will still get to make decisions and be served, but there will be someone else you must consider.

So let me ask you this: How are you serving right now to prepare you for marriage? Are you able and willing to cook for others, rearrange your schedule to be able to spend time with them, or run errands for them? Girlie, if you can't even cook, keep your fish alive, or rearrange plans for someone you enjoy spending time with, what makes you think marriage will be easier? I do not want to scare you or put a bad taste in your mouth. I merely want to open your eyes to the reality of putting others first. And I know you have it in you. God has created us with a nurturing nature that wants to care for and serve others. So are you ready to put someone else first in your life? I have heard this: your marriage will be as good as you are selfless.

In Ephesians 5:21, Paul tells husbands and wives, "Submit to one another out of reverence for Christ." Paul then goes further and tells wives to submit to their husbands as they submit to the Lord. Wow! That is a lot, but what does that really mean? It means to willingly let go of an idea or what you would have chosen as the best solution for a problem and be able to respectfully accept your husband's decision, trusting that he is going to the Lord for help. Don't get me wrong. It does not mean that you become passive and silent. Marriage is a team effort. It just means you are trusting your husband to make the best decision after considering God's, his, and your input. You see, when you marry a man, you also submit to his vision and therefore trust that he knows where God is taking both of you. Remember Eve? God made her to be a helper. That means women are to come alongside men to help them achieve the mission God has placed in them. I am not saying that you give up your own dreams and desires but rather that you submit to the way he is paving for both of your lives since you are now *one.*

Let's dig deeper into marriage. Besides servanthood, marriage is also a symbol of Christ and the church. Ephesians 5:25 tells husbands to love their wives as Christ loves the church. Marriage is a covenant between a man and a woman as Christ made a covenant with us when He died for us. God feels so strongly about marriage that he used it as a metaphor for Christ's love for us and to illustrate its significance. Marriage is a holy union and a living symbol. Think about it. Christ died as a living sacrifice and therefore made us pure in God's eyes. In marriage, you make a covenant with your husband, and both of you start a purification process that makes you more Christlike.

Is This Guy Husband Material?

Now that you have a little bit more revelation about what marriage is, you might be asking this: How can I discern if a guy is husband material? Here are some starter questions:

- Is he a believer who has a relationship with God and a prayer life?
- Is he plugged in at a church where he is serving and surrounded by community?
- Is he walking in his calling with a vision of where he is going?
- Does he have noble character? Does he respect you and treat you with manners?
- Does he wash you with the water of the Word? Does he challenge you by pointing out what the Bible says about certain situations to exhort you in love and make you pure (Eph. 5:25–26)?
- Does he make you want to know more about God and walk closer with Him?
- Is he intentional about presenting you without spot or blemish? Is he protecting your purity (Eph. 5:27)?
- Does he treat his parents with respect and honor?

- Is your love based on a friendship? Do you love spending time with him without being physical? Marriage is a commitment, and you won't feel butterflies every day.
- Are you attracted just to his looks or to his looks and his brain? Can you have a conversation with him?
- Is he clear with his intentions, or is he vague about the whole situation? You do not have time for someone who does not know your worth or what he wants. Remember, God is not the author of confusion, and indecision is a decision.

CHAPTER TEN

The Husband

At this point, you might be asking: How do I know who the right guy is? When the time comes, you will meet your husband, and you will know. I believe God has someone specifically for you to walk this life with, but I also know God has given us free will. That being said, you have to get to a point in which you are open to what God has for you. You might have a list of requirements for your future husband, but make sure you leave room for God's list. You might even be asking if you should have a list. I have heard different stories. Some people made a list with God, and their spouse met 100 percent of the bullet points. For other people, that was not the case. They didn't settle; rather, they were open to what God thought was best. You see, if you decide to write a list, I would suggest having a light grip on it and being open to what God has for you. For example, just because you want a guy with light eyes does not mean you should be closed off to someone with brown eyes. The list should be there to remind you of what you deserve—a godly man who loves God and has character and values. The list should not be full of physical attributes since looks are not the foundation of a good marriage. Will you trust God with your desires? He never disappoints.

God spoke to me about this through an experience. I went hiking with a friend, and we were determined to find a certain pond everyone was talking about. We kept walking in circles and running across creeks. I assumed they were the pond and asked in disappointment, "So this is the pond?" Then someone said, "No, this is a creek." So we kept walking. We kept running into creeks, and I kept asking the same question. Finally, a man said, "Just keep going. You can't miss it! You'll know when you find it." And it hit me. That's how it is sometimes in relationships. We keep coming across distractions and counterfeit relationships in our lives and get disappointed, thinking, "Wow! Is this what I've been waiting for?" Girlie, I believe that when you find that person, you will *know* and won't be able to miss it. And I don't mean you will know based on looks alone but based on that person's spirit. Be encouraged. From the beginning, God has already planned the end.

Let's look at Isaac and Rebekah's story (Gen. 24). Isaac was Abraham's son. Abraham did not want him to marry a Canaanite woman since those women were idol worshipers and Isaac would therefore be unequally yoked. So Abraham sent one of his servants to his homeland to find a wife for Isaac. Abraham knew it was time for his son to take on the role of a husband. Are you ready to take on the role of a wife? Have you asked God what season of life you are in? You see, when it is God's time, your husband will find you. Abraham did not send his servant one year before or later than the appointment time. He was connected to God's timing. The second aspect to note is that Abraham had total confidence and faith that God would provide.

Once the servant got to Abraham's homeland, he started praying for a confirmation from God. The Bible says he was not even done praying in his heart when his prayer was answered and Rebekah came on the scene (Gen. 24:45). God has planned to answer your prayers even before you pray them. If that is not mind-blowing, I don't know what is. The Creator of the universe placed the desire in your heart and has planned to fulfill it since the beginning of time. The Bible says God has known the end from the beginning (Isa.

46:10). Girlie, He is the Alpha and the Omega, the first and the last, the beginning and the end (Rev. 22:13). What can get past Him? Be encouraged!

Next, Rebekah gave Abraham's servant and his camels water and invited him to stay. The servant then told the family why he had come, and they agreed to let Rebekah go and blessed her. Most importantly, Rebekah agreed to go. As they reached Negev, Isaac's home, she jumped off the camel and asked if Isaac was the person she saw from afar. The Bible does not say this, but I believe she hurried because she thought this man was good-looking.

We can gather several key points from this story about discerning when it is your season and whether the person is right for you.

1. **Are you trusting God completely instead of trying to make this happen on your own?** Isaac and Rebekah trusted completely by letting the servant (who was being led by God) arrange this marriage. God knows what is best for you.

2. **Are you in sync with God's timing?** Abraham as a dad recognized that his son was ready. When God sees you, does He see that you are ready?

3. **Does the person have noble character?** We don't get much insight about Isaac, but the servant did assess Rebekah's character. I believe that instead of trying to find the right person, we as women should start becoming the right person. So let's look at Rebekah's attributes. First, she was a servant. She immediately greeted the servant and offered him a drink of water. She was also a hard worker. She offered to give water to his camels, which is not an easy thing to do. Camels can drink up to 25 gallons of water after a week of travel. Imagine how much water she had to draw from the well. Assess the person and their actions.

4. **Are others around you confirming that the relationship is from God?** In the Bible, we see how Rebekah's family agreed to the plan by trusting that the arrangement was from God.

It is important to bring that person around community and family. During the time of courtship, they are the ones who can see red flags and catch anything that is not for you.

5. **Do you have peace about it?** Rebekah, her family, and the servant all had peace. Even Isaac did not doubt. Do not rely solely on emotions, but do remember that the Holy Spirit can nudge you. If you are being prayerful and feel uneasy, remember that God is not a God of confusion. If the guy is not being clear, ask for clarity. Isaac did not play games with Rebekah. Once he met her, he immediately made her his wife. He recognized her value and worth.

6. **Are your parents or those close to you blessing the relationship?** We see this when Rebekah's family blesses her to leave to meet Isaac. If your parents are not believers or not walking rightly, things might be different. Choose wisdom and seek elders around you who can help you evaluate the relationship.

7. **Are you physically attracted to this person?** Hear me out. I am not saying physical attraction is the most important aspect. The Bible tells us that "charm is deceptive, and beauty is fleeting; but a woman who fears the LORD is to be praised" (Prov. 31:30). But I believe you have to be attracted to the person in some way. Either that will happen instantly, or he will grow on you. The Bible tells us that Rebekah was beautiful and that she dismounted from her camel when she saw Isaac, showing him respect. Come with me and stretch this a little further. I like to think this reaction was also due to how attractive he was, although we will never know until we get to heaven. I do want to make something clear. I do not believe God will make you marry someone you are not attracted to. He is intentional and specific, so do not settle.

Keep in mind that these are only pointers. Once you are in this stage, let the Holy Spirit guide you. He is the best counselor.

Ending Prayer

Father, thank You for the gift of marriage You have for me. I pray that You would start revealing Your image of marriage and start molding and shaping my heart to be ready for it. I lift up my future husband, Lord. I pray that he would be rooted and grounded in love and your Word. I declare that he is a mighty man of God who is both physically and mentally pure. Thank You for protecting him and removing any distraction from his life. Thank You, God, for that anointed time when we will meet, and I declare that no plan of the enemy will thwart Your timing.

Conclusion

We have gotten to the end of this book, and I hope that by now you have jotted down ways you can partner with the Holy Spirit to enjoy and maximize your season of singleness. Even though I encourage you to work on all the areas I covered in this book, I do not want you to base God's timing on the status of a checklist. Girlie, your husband is not a reward for your behavior, your striving, or how well you go through these points. The Bible says God's ways are higher than ours. It says that God is not slow to keep His promises, but He is patient so no one will perish. What does that mean? He is orchestrating everything behind the scenes in *due time*. You see, God is a good Father, and He delights in fulfilling promises to you, but He knows when you are ultimately ready. He is not trying to trick you or make you strive for things. Would you take His invitation to rest in Him? I'm not saying that being proactive and taking steps to better yourself and prepare yourself is a bad idea, but do so from a posture of trust, rest, and patience. God's got you. I'm praying for God to meet you where you are and to bring joy, peace, and contentment in this season.

With love,
Janelle

Special Thanks

Wow! Never in my life did I think I would write a book. I want to thank God for using me as a vessel to empower women and encourage them in their single season. This book is proof that He uses everything for our good and does not waste anything. Mom, thank you for showing me what it looks like to have a relationship with Jesus, for surrendering everything to Him, and for being an example of how to be obedient to God. Dad, Andres, Nicolle—thank you for always supporting me.

Carolina, Kayla, Rachel, Gaby, and Cari—thank you for always cheering me on in the ups and downs of each season, for not giving up on my vision, and for speaking life into me. I love you girls. Also, special thanks to graphic designer and jack of all trades Carolina Caicedo who took the headshot. For more information, contact her at www.carolinacaicedo.com.

Thanks to Lucid Books for believing in this book. It would have been impossible without you. Finally, thank you to Michael McIntyre and the team for reminding me of who I am in Christ and challenging me to live the life He has planned for me. For more information on their life-changing trainings and to start living the life God planned for you, visit www.michaelpmcintyre.com/nextlevel.

CPSIA information can be obtained
at www.ICGtesting.com
Printed in the USA
BVHW040859280821
615434BV00010B/1296